W9-BOA-032

Discover Southern New Hampshire

Discover Southern New Hampshire

AMC Guide to the
Best Hiking, Biking, and Paddling

Jerry and Marcy Monkman

APPALACHIAN MOUNTAIN CLUB BOOKS
BOSTON, MASSACHUSETTS

Cover Photograph: Jerry and Marcy Monkman
All photographs by the author unless otherwise noted
Cover Design: Belinda Desher
Book Design: Mac & Dent

Distributed by The Globe Pequot Press, Inc., Guilford, CT

Library of Congress Cataloging-in-Publication Data is available.

ISBN 1-929173-15-6

The paper used in this publication meets the minimum requirements of the American National Standard for Information Sciences—Permanence of Paper for Printed Library Materials, ANSI Z39.48–1984. ∞

**Due to changes in conditions,
use of the information in this book
is at the sole risk of the user.**

Printed on recycled paper using soy-based inks.
Printed in the United States of America.

10 9 8 7 6 5 4 3 2 1   01 02 03 04 05 06

contents

introduction

WE HAVE LIVED IN SOUTHERN NEW HAMPSHIRE for almost a decade, but we have spent much of that time elsewhere, photographing and exploring the better-known wild places of New England: Acadia, the White Mountains, and the Northern Forest. When we began our research for this book we knew we would find scenic coastline to explore and fragrant forests to wander through, but we were surprised and delighted to find such a wide variety of wild places and adventure experiences so close to home. While there are no true alpine summits in southern New Hampshire, we found it is still possible to stand high above the valleys on an open ridge top in August and feel a cool breeze across our faces as we gazed at the White and Green Mountains. More important, we often found ourselves alone on the trail, stepping over moose tracks as we made our way through dark hemlock forests punctuated by showy mountain laurel.

This solitude was a welcome reward for our travels, but just as rewarding was experiencing the thrill of rushing whitewater on the Sugar River, floating past basking painted turtles on Grafton Pond, and watching deer and red fox in the hidden coves of Portsmouth Harbor. Whether hiking, biking, or paddling, we were constantly reminded of New Hampshire's agricultural past, as we found old stone walls, cellar holes, or stone dams on almost every trip in this book. These artifacts were especially evident while mountain biking, because many bike trails follow old town roads that are no longer in use, linking New Hampshire's historical past to its outdoor adventure present. In fact, the old roads and newer single-track in state parks such as Pisgah, Pawtuckaway, and Bear Brook provide some of the best mountain biking in New England. While there are too many trails, ponds, and rivers to include them all in this book, we feel the fifty trips described here explore some of the best nooks and crannies that New Hampshire has to offer.

In addition to using this guide, you can find more great places in southern New Hampshire by joining one or more of the local organizations dedicated to maintaining trails and protecting watersheds (see appendix B). Participating in trail maintenance or river clean-up days is an excellent way to give back to the land and meet people who know the local area intimately. The more time you spend in the wild places of southern New Hampshire, the more you will discover and the more you will want to protect them. Let us know what you find by sending us an e-mail at nature@ecophotography.com.

acknowledgments

THIS IS THE THIRD BOOK in our "Discover" series, and while we found the work to be a little easier than the first time around, we still depended on many others to help us create the best guidebook possible. First and foremost, we would like to thank the staff at AMC Books—Beth Krusi, Blake Maher, Belinda Desher, and Laurie O'Reilly. Their editorial, production, and marketing guidance are instrumental in the success of these guides. Larry Garland, the AMC's cartographer, also deserves a special thank-you for his persistence in converting our scribbles into readable and useful maps. Carol Tyler has proved once again that she can skillfully turn our endless word-processing documents and spreadsheets into a well-designed, easy-to-read book.

While we often enjoyed "Discovering" southern New Hampshire on our own, we could not have found all of the great places in this book without the advice and support of friends and people devoted to the protection of New Hampshire's wild places. We would especially like to thank Rosemary Conroy of the Society for the Protection of New Hampshire Forests; Margaret Watkins, Dick Lord, and Sonya Gonzales of the Lamprey River Advisory Council; and the many friends who joined us on the trail: John and Judy Muller, Pete Devlin, Mark and Ola Russell, Mike and Peter Herlihy, Karen and Kelly Meyers, Karen Mucci, Ty Wivell, Deborah Kendall, and Ned and Jean Therrien. Once again, we completely depended on the New Hampshire paddling chapter of the AMC for advice and guidance on river paddling. Trip leaders who provided excellent information and support were Mike Jacobs, Dennis Belliveau, Atilla and Jackie Farkas, and Bruce Healy. We would especially like to thank Prijon Kayaks and John and Mitchell at Canoe King in Ossipee.

Most important, we would like to once again thank our families for their unconditional loving support of all we do.

locator map

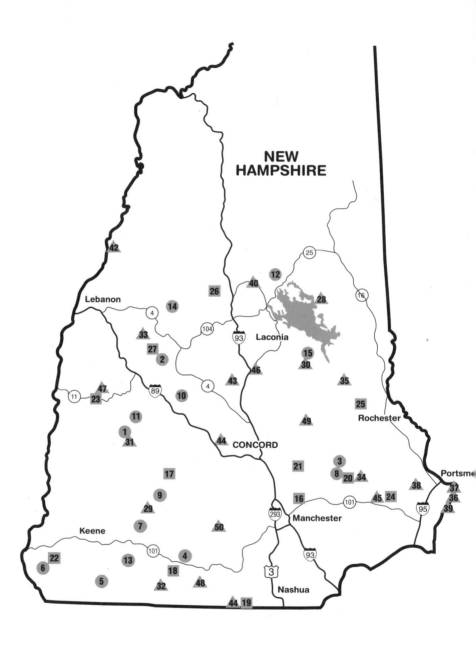

Trips

Hiking ●

Biking ▪

Paddling ▲

LEGEND

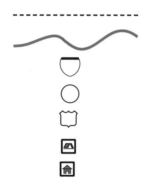

Trip

Alternate Trip

Water

Interstate Route

US Route

State Route

Tentsite/Campground

Hut/Cabin

Shelter

Parking

Direction of Travel

Scenic View

1

Southern New Hampshire
basic information

SOUTHERN NEW HAMPSHIRE has a subtle beauty of rolling hills and sparkling lakes that draws tourists from around the world. Visitors to the area have been seeking the heights of peaks like Monadnock or the cool breezes of Lake Winnipesauke and the Isles of Shoals since the 1850s. Today adventure seekers come to southern New Hampshire for its superb mountain biking, its huge variety of paddling opportunities, and its network of hiking trails that manage to offer great views while winding their way through a diverse forest that has reclaimed the land from nineteenth-century sheep and dairy farms. Close to Boston, and home to New Hampshire's biggest cities, the southern part of the state has a surprisingly large number of wild places that provide homes for moose, otters, bald eagles, loons, and bears. Unfortunately, southern New Hampshire is one of the most sprawl-threatened parts of New England, but as you will find while embarking on the trips in this book, there are still large stretches of forests and river corridors that provide important habitat links between all parts of the state and the rest of New England.

Chapters 4 through 8 of this book give detailed descriptions of hiking, biking, and paddling trips, from one-hour excursions to all-day adventures, while chapter 9 provides information for participating in other activities. The rest of this introductory chapter provides some basic information you can use to get started on your visit to southern New Hampshire.

Climate

Southern New Hampshire has typical northern New England weather with five seasons: mud, black fly, summer, fall, and winter. On a more serious note, spring is generally wet and cool, with day-time highs in the low forties through the low sixties and lows in the twenties, thirties, and forties. Trails are generally too muddy for bikes before June, but spring is the best time for paddling southern New Hampshire's rivers—spring rain and snowmelt add up to create excellent conditions. Biting black flies are at their worst in May and early June, which is when we typically stay near the coast and its sea breezes. Summer highs range from the low seventies into the nineties, while lows are generally in the fifties and sixties. While summer in New Hampshire sees a little more rain than spring, the rain is more likely to come in the form of afternoon showers and thunderstorms as opposed to day-long bouts of drizzle. Fall is cool and crisp with temperatures similar to those in spring. Precipitation can vary widely and change quickly—it is hurricane season—so check the forecast before heading out for a long day. Winter is of course cold and snowy, with the immediate coast prone to bouts of freezing rain and southwestern New Hampshire prone to huge snowfalls of two feet or more. Daytime highs are usually in the twenties or thirties, with lows in the teens. Current weather forecasts can be obtained by calling the National Weather Service at 603-225-5191. Many websites also carry up-to-date weather information (www.wunderground.com).

Getting There

Southern New Hampshire is served by several major airlines and bus services. Manchester is the fastest-growing airport in the region and is one of the most convenient airports in New England. Bus service is provided to major New Hampshire cities by C & J Trailways

(800-258-7111, www.cjtrailways.com) and Concord Trailways (800-639-3317, www.concordtrailways.com). Major driving routes include I-93, I-95, NH 101, NH 9, NH 4, and US 202.

Lodging

Like most of New Hampshire, the region is well served by the tourism industry: there are countless hotels, bed-and-breakfasts, and campgrounds in the area. Appendix C to this book has a campground listing as well as resources for finding other accommodations.

New Hampshire State Parks and Forests Information

The trips in this book pass through a variety of public and private lands, including state parks, state forests, and private preserves owned by various conservation groups. Contact information for private preserves can be found in the trip descriptions that use those preserves. For state lands, see the listing of parks and forests in appendix D. For general information about New Hampshire state parks, you can contact:

New Hampshire Division of Parks and Recreation
P.O. Box 1856
172 Pembroke Road
Concord, NH 03302
603-271-3556
www.nhparks.state.nh.us

To make camping reservations at a state park, call 603-271-3628.

Fees

Most state parks charge a day-use fee of $3 or less per person that is usually in effect from Memorial Day through Columbus Day, but this varies from park to park. A season pass for all state parks (including weekday access to Wallis Sands and Hampton State Beaches) can be purchased for $50. Children under twelve are free. Camping fees vary from park to park and are usually in the range of $12 to $15 per site.

Universal Access

The state park listings in the appendix detail the accessibility of each park. Rhododendron State Park has one of the state's best accessible woodland trails (see trip #5).

Some other universally accessible outdoor destinations are as follows:

- Northwood Meadows Pioneer Park in the Merrimack Valley Region. This 600-acre park is currently being developed to be as universally accessible as possible. There are a number of hiking trails, some of which are wheelchair-accessible.

- Adams Point, by the Jackson Estuarine Research Laboratory, off Durham Point Road in Durham. An observation platform here is ideal for bird watching.

- Sandy Point, the salt marsh in Stratham on Great Bay, has a 1,600-foot boardwalk that is accessible for those with limited mobility.

- The "Garden of the Senses" at the Urban Forestry Center in Portsmouth is particularly recommended for the sight impaired.

Emergencies

In an emergency situation, you should call 911, as New Hampshire has a statewide 911 system in place. Backcountry accidents and search-and-rescue situations can also be reported to the New Hampshire State Police at 800-852-3411.

Choosing Your Trip

The fifty hiking, biking, and paddling trips in this book provide a variety of outdoor experiences. Before heading out on the trail or on the water, you should decide what the focus of your trip is (play-boating, mountain views, wildlife watching, and so forth). You should also decide how strenuous a trip you and your group are willing and able to complete. The highlight chart in chapter 3 is an easy-to-follow listing of all the trips, including their difficulty, length, and trip highlights. Once you have narrowed down your choices, read the detailed trip descriptions in the individual hiking, biking, and paddling chapters to get a better idea of what the trip entails and what you might encounter.

Hunting Season

Hunting is allowed in many state parks, state forests, and on private property in southern New Hampshire. Hunting accidents are rare in the state, but everyone in your group, including dogs, should wear at least one piece of blaze-orange clothing during hunting season. Hunting seasons are set by the New Hampshire Fish and Game Department and are posted on its website, www.wildlife.state.nh.us/hunting.html. In general, the various hunting seasons are as follows:

- Deer: archery—mid-September through mid-December; muzzleloader—end of October through first week of November; regular firearms (shotguns and rifles)—early November through early December

- Black bear: early September through early December

- Moose: nine days, starting on the third Saturday in October

- Turkey: archery—mid-September through mid-December; archery and shotgun—May

- Birds and small mammals: usually early October through December

Don't Drink the Water

While the water in many New Hampshire streams is probably safe to drink, there is no way to tell a safe water source from a contaminated one. Even water bubbling up from a spring can contain bacteria, viruses, or protozoa that can cause illness. If you are just out for the day, the easiest thing to do is just bring enough water with you. If you are camping or prefer to fill up on an "as needed" basis, use one of the following procedures for purifying your water:

- Boiling: Boiling water for one to three minutes is a surefire way to kill any diseases that may be in it. The downside is having to set up a stove and then wait for the water to boil and cool down before drinking.

- Filtering: Using a portable water filter is a convenient way to get potable water. There are several different kinds of filters; some use glass, carbon, or ceramic elements to strain the nasties out of the water. These take care of bacteria and protozoa, but not viruses (which are rare in the American backcountry), and are fine for New Hampshire—just make sure the filter element has a pore size of 0.2 micron or smaller. If you want extra protection, buy a filter that also passes the water through a layer of iodine, which will kill viruses.

- Chemical treatments: Dropping a few tablets of a chemical purifier such as Potable Aqua is a simple, lightweight water purification solution. The downside is that your water will have an unpleasant iodine taste. This can be covered up somewhat with powdered drinks such as Gatorade or Tang. Also, chemical treatments cannot kill the *Cryptospordium* cyst, which can cause flulike symptoms, including diarrhea and severe bloating. We carry Potable Aqua in our first-aid kit for emergency purposes on day hikes when we don't want to carry the extra weight of a filter.

Backcountry Camping

There are not many backcountry camping opportunities in southern New Hampshire, so it is best to assume it is not allowed. There are a few exceptions. You will find some remote canoe camping sites in

Pillsbury State Park and along the Connecticut River. (See trips #31 and #42 for information). Also, a few "walk-in" sites near the Appalachian Mountain Club (AMC) Cardigan Lodge give the feel of backcountry camping, but most sites are within 0.5 mile of the parking area. (Call the AMC at 603-466-2721 for information.) It is also possible to camp along some of the long-distance trails in the state, such as the Metacomet-Monadnock Trail and the Wapack Trail. These trails cross quite a bit of private property, however, so permission for camping must be secured ahead of time in most instances. The best bet for a multiday hike in southern New Hampshire is probably the three- or four-day trip along the Monadnock–Sunapee Greenway. Good information and a trail guide for this 50-mile-long trail are available from:

> Monadnock–Sunapee Greenway Trail Club
> P.O. Box 164
> Marlow, NH 03456
> www.msgtc.org

Protect the Resource!

The second-growth forests and newly clean rivers of southern New Hampshire are beautiful examples of how wild places can be reborn. If these places are to remain healthy, it is imperative that everyone learn and adhere to Leave No Trace principles. These principles were developed by the National Outdoor Leadership School in order to promote and inspire responsible outdoor recreation. How we use the forest now determines what the forest will be like in the future. Whether you are hiking, biking, or paddling, follow these principles:

Plan ahead and prepare

When going into the backcountry, plan a day that you know everyone in your group can finish. Be prepared for unexpected events by having extra food, water, and clothing. A well-planned day will prevent the need for an unnecessary night out in the woods, when you may be forced to build fires and trample delicate vegetation. Keep your group size to ten or less, splitting into smaller groups if necessary. (This is required in designated wilderness areas.) Try to avoid travel in wet and muddy conditions, and use extra care when in the delicate alpine zone. Planning ahead also means confirming that you are traveling and/or camping in an area where it is legal to do so.

Camp and travel on durable surfaces

When hiking, try to stay on trails and rocks. When you are on a trail, stay in the center of the trail, even when it is wet and muddy. Use your boots! Trails are hardened sites where use should be concentrated. Avoid contributing to the widening and braiding of trails. Hiking off-trail into pristine areas is allowed in most places (check individual park regulations) but requires greater understanding and effort. (It is especially discouraged above treeline.) First consider if hiking off-trail is necessary. If you feel it is, use durable surfaces such as rock, gravel, or grasses. Spread out your group, take different routes, and avoid places where unofficial "social" trails are just beginning to show. While mountain biking, always stay on the trail. Camping in the backcountry, if allowed, should be at designated sites, at sites that have already been impacted, or 200 feet from trails and water sources. Avoid sites that have seen moderate impact; your visit could create more damage.

Dispose of waste properly

Pack out all that you bring in. This includes any and all food you may drop while eating. Urinate at least 200 yards from any water source and pack out your used toilet paper. To dispose of solid human waste in the backcountry, dig an individual "cat hole" at least 200 yards from a trail or water source. Organic topsoil is preferable to sandy mineral soil. The hole should be 4 to 8 inches deep and about 6 inches in diameter. After use, mix some soil into the cat hole with a stick and cover with the remainder of the soil. Disguise the hole by covering it with leaves or other brush. Pack out your toilet paper in an odor-proof bag. It is especially important not to pollute near any watercourse, as it probably leads to a campground or town water source.

Leave what you find

Leave all natural and historical items as you find them. There is much human history in southern New Hampshire that should be left for future visitors to enjoy. Eating a few blueberries on a hike or adding a wild mushroom to a camp dinner is okay, but it may be illegal to harvest any forest product for commercial purposes without a permit from the state parks and forests. Before picking any wild edibles, consider the number of other people who might be using the area and decide if you will be negatively affecting an important food source for wildlife.

Minimize campfire impacts

Use a lightweight, backpacking stove when in the backcountry. Try to build campfires only in designated fire pits in campgrounds and picnic areas.

Respect wildlife

Remain quiet while in the backcountry, and give wildlife enough space so that they feel secure. While watching animals, if you notice them changing their behavior, it is most likely because you are too close; back off and give them space. Avoid nesting or calving sites and never attempt to feed any wildlife, even those cute little red squirrels. For low-impact wildlife-watching tips, visit Watchable Wildlife's website, www.watchablewildlife.org.

Be considerate of other visitors

Stay quiet. Refrain from using cell phones and radios. When hiking, take rests on the side of the trail so that other hikers do not have to walk around you. When on the water, remember that sound carries a long, long way.

You can learn more about the Leave No Trace program by contacting the organization:

LNT Inc.
P.O. Box 997
Boulder, CO 80306
www.lnt.org

A good book for learning more about ethics in the backcountry is *Backwoods Ethics: Environmental Issues for Hikers and Campers* by Laura and Guy Waterman.

2
history

ALL OF NEW HAMPSHIRE is a dramatic example of how the natural landscape can change over time. Only 150 years ago, more than 50 percent of the state had been deforested for agriculture, much of it for sheep pasture. Today, after more than a century of regrowth, 85 percent of the state is covered in forest, but even a short walk through the woods will uncover reminders of the state's agricultural past: stone walls, cellar holes, and apple trees in the middle of the woods. Of course, New Hampshire's landscape has a much more distant history as well, and while on the trips in this book you will notice evidence of the crashing of continental plates that occurred more than 400 million years ago. You will also walk over mountains made of granite formed by magma deep within the earth and paddle in kettle holes created by glaciers during the last ice age. This chapter provides a brief summary of the forces that have shaped what is now southern New Hampshire.

Geological History

Five hundred million years ago, all of New Hampshire lay under a vast ancient ocean known as the proto-Atlantic. The North American continent ended around the present-day eastern border of Vermont. Over millions of years, sedimentary rock formed at the bottom of this ancient ocean. Between 500 million and 300 million years ago, multiple mountain-building events took place as the European and African continents merged with the North American continental plate. First, what is known as the Taconian event created an ancient mountain range. As ancient Europe moved across the Atlantic, it pushed a volcanic chain of islands, much like Japan and the Philippines, into the North American continent. The pressures of this collision transformed sedimentary rocks such as sandstone, shale, and limestone into much harder metamorphic rocks such as quartzite, schist, gneiss, and marble. By the end of this collision, around 435 million years ago, new mountains stood in Vermont and far western New Hampshire. The hills west of Keene and in the Lebanon-Hanover area date to this time frame. The rest of what would become New Hampshire, however, still lay at the bottom of the ocean.

Much of the mountains built during the Taconian event eroded away into the proto-Atlantic, creating new layers of sedimentary rock over the future state. Between 335 and 375 million years ago, the European and African plates eventually collided with North America in what is known as the Acadian mountain-building cycle, or Acadian Orogeny. This event created a mountain range, called the Acadian Mountains, throughout New Hampshire. Again, sedimentary rocks were metamorphosed into much harder rocks, the most resistant of which are still visible today and are known as Littleton schist. The Presidential Range in the White Mountains consists of Littleton schist, which was much more resistant to erosion than other rocks. This schist extends south to southwestern New Hampshire and is the primary component of Mount Monadnock and Pack Monadnock. Even the rocky shoreline in Rye is composed of schist from this period. According to this picture of history, most of New Hampshire was once part of Africa or Europe.

The mountain building did not end with the Acadian Orogeny, however. As the continents once again separated to re-form the Atlantic Ocean about 200 million years ago, Earth's crust was stretched and fractured, allowing magma to bubble up from deep within the planet. This is when most of New Hampshire's granite was formed in underground magma plutons and aboveground volcanic

lava flows. The most common rocks from this era include Moat vol-
canics (still seen on Moat Mountain), Conway granite, Mount Osce-
ola granite (most of Mount Chocorua), and Winnipesaukee granite.
In southern New Hampshire the granite from this event can be
found on peaks such as Red Hill in Sandwich, Pawtuckaway Mountain in Nottingham, and Mount Cardigan in Bristol.

Millions of years of erosion have taken place since these
mountain-building events, leaving behind a landscape with a complex composition. Sedimentary rocks have completely disappeared
from the New Hampshire terrain, leaving a mixture of igneous rocks,
such as granite and basalt, and metamorphic schists and gneisses.
Because schists are the most durable of these rocks, they make up
the tallest peaks, while granite is more common on lower peaks.
Over the past 2 or 3 million years, much of the erosion in New England has occurred during periods of heavy glaciation. During this
time frame, there have been several periods of glaciation, known as
ice ages, when all of New Hampshire was covered in a layer of ice,
sometimes more than a mile thick.

The last ice age, known as the Wisconsin glaciation, peaked
around 18,000 years ago when a continental ice sheet reached as far
south as Long Island. All of southern New Hampshire was completely covered with ice, and the smooth, rounded peaks of the
region are a result of glacial scouring. Grooves in the rock surface of
these summits are known as glacial striations. The ice age left other
features as well, most notably drumlins and kettle holes. Drumlins
are made of glacial till that was shaped into streamlined hills by the
moving ice of a glacier. Many of the lower hills in the region west of
I-93 in New Hampshire are drumlins. Kettle holes are depressions in
the earth that were created when big blocks of ice buried in glacial
deposits melted over time. These kettle holes often become small
ponds or bogs. Mud Pond in Fox State Forest is a good example of
a glacial kettle hole.

The ice completely retreated from New Hampshire at some
point between 12,000 and 14,000 years ago. For a while, the area
resembled the high Arctic, where only lichens and small tundra
plants could survive. Remnants of this tundra community still exist
farther north in the White Mountains above treeline. As the climate
slowly warmed, the composition of plant species began to change.
Conifers such as spruce and fir first grew in the recently thawed soil.

Over time, hardwoods moved in as well, first birch and aspen, then beech and maple and oak. About 3,000 years ago, the current make-up of forests was reached, with northern hardwood and oak-hickory forests common at lower elevations, and boreal forests dominant above 3,000 feet.

Human History

Most of New England probably became suitable for human habitation once the ice retreated around 12,000 years ago. There is very little evidence of early human habitation from this period, but at that time the area was similar to the Arctic in climate, and it is impossible to determine whether people lived year-round in the area or just passed through at certain times of year. By 6000 B.C., Native Americans had begun to settle in the more hospitable climes of river valleys. In southern New Hampshire this meant the areas around the Connecticut and Merrimack Rivers.

Just prior to first contact with Europeans, various bands of the Abenaki Indians (a subculture of the Algonkians who lived throughout the Northeast) lived in southern New Hampshire, cultivating corn to supplement a diet of wild game, fish, and native plants. The most notable of these were the Cowasuck, "people of the white pines," who lived in the upper Connecticut River watershed, and the Penacook, who were centered near Concord but were spread out over much of southern New Hampshire and north-central Massachusetts. While an accurate assessment of the population of these tribes is difficult, they probably numbered between 10,000 and 25,000 in the southern part of the state. They lived in family groups, usually descended from a common female ancestor, but the Abenakis were also connected beyond their immediate families to extended families, bands, and villages. Their leaders, known as sachems or sagamores, often connected these bands and villages together, allocating hunting territories and conducting diplomacy with other peoples, including Europeans when they began arriving in the sixteenth and seventeenth centuries.

When southern New Hampshire was settled by the British in the early seventeenth century, the Abenaki tribes had already been greatly reduced in number due to epidemics of introduced diseases from Europe, the most deadly of which was smallpox. As much as

75 percent of some Native tribes in New England died from these diseases, which were spread primarily through contact with the Dutch and French fur traders who had begun trading in the area during the sixteenth century. Most of the remaining Abenakis fled to Quebec in the early eighteenth century as a result of white persecution—most notably a massacre along the Baker River near Plymouth in 1712. Today the largest communities of Abenakis are in eastern Maine and Quebec.

The first recorded reference to what is now New Hampshire was made by the Italian explorer Giovanni da Verrazano, who sailed along the New England coast in 1524. The New Hampshire coast was most likely known to European traders and fishermen even before that time, but it was not until the 1620s that permanent settlements were established. At that time Captain John Mason, former governor of Newfoundland, received a grant of land from the English Crown that included the area between the Merrimack and Piscataqua Rivers. He called this land New Hampshire after his family homestead in Hampshire, England. Mason never visited his extensive landholdings in the New World, but in 1630 he sent Captain Walter Neal and a small crew to the Piscataqua watershed to establish a settlement. They chose a piece of land in what is now Portsmouth to start their colony, which they christened Strawbery Banke. Shortly after Strawbery Banke, later renamed Portsmouth, was settled, the town of Dover was established farther upriver.

By the end of the 1630s, the towns of Hampton and Exeter had also been established, and it was these four towns of the Piscataqua watershed that dominated New Hampshire culture and politics for the next 100 years. During this time, New Hampshire thrived economically by exporting fur, fish, and timber to Europe and the West Indies, and by 1706 the last virgin forests in the Piscataqua basin had been cut. Of course, settlement moved inland over time, and by the American Revolution, much of southern New Hampshire had been settled, with most of the interior consisting of family farms that produced their own meat, vegetables, and wool as well as cash crops such as cider, cheese, and timber. The forces that would most dramatically alter the southern New Hampshire landscape were still decades and an ocean away.

In the early nineteenth century, Portuguese aristocrats bred the merino sheep. The merino's fleece was used to create very soft, high-quality wool that was in great demand worldwide. The Portuguese banned the export of merino sheep, and this ban remained in effect until Napoleon conquered Portugal in 1809. In 1810 William Jarvis, the American consul to Portugal, imported 4,000 merinos to his farm in Weathersfield, Vermont. It turned out that Jarvis had good timing: after the War of 1812, the U.S. government used tariffs to make the importing of English woolens cost-prohibitive. For the next thirty years, farmers in Vermont and New Hampshire cleared more and more land for pasture in order to cash in on the booming domestic wool market. By 1840 there were more than 600,000 sheep in New Hampshire, with more than two-thirds of the southern New Hampshire landscape converted from forest into pasture.

A majority of the stone walls in southern New Hampshire were built to keep sheep in their pastures—the walls you will now encounter on most hikes and bike rides through the region's forests. Sheep farming reached its peak in New Hampshire in 1840. In the effort to produce as much wool as possible, farmers overgrazed much of their pastures, and the thin New Hampshire soils could not keep up. The least productive farms were abandoned quickly, because they could not compete with new, more productive farms farther west. After the Civil War, even more farms were abandoned as many families moved on to farm the richer soils of the Midwest. While farms are still common throughout southern New Hampshire, most of the forest has grown back, and is once again home to bears and moose, beavers and otters.

It was during the wool boom that New Hampshire's textile industry grew to worldwide prominence—the Amoskeag Mill in Manchester was the largest mill complex in the world at the time— and this dramatically changed the flow of the rivers in the region, as dams and canals were built to produce energy and ease transportation. Most of the mills from this time period are closed now, but reminders of their heyday can still be found while paddling the area's rivers—breached dams, stone tailraces, and brick mill buildings.

While textiles and lumber ruled the state's pre–twentieth-century economy, the tourism that is now such a big part of the job base got its start in the nineteenth century. The tourists who then visited southern New Hampshire headed to places still popular today, such as Lake Winnipesaukee and the seacoast, including the Isles of Shoals. The ancestors of today's outdoor adventure seekers often found their way to Mount Monadnock, however, which is shared by the towns of Dublin and Jaffrey. While the first recorded ascent of Mount Monadnock was in 1725, in the 1820s the mountain began to see a steady flow of hikers, most notably Ralph Waldo Emerson and Henry David Thoreau. The popular White Arrow Trail was constructed in 1854, and by 1860 overnight guests were staying alongside this trail at the Mountain House, which was later replaced by the Halfway House. The site of the Halfway House, which burned down in 1954, is still visible to hikers on the White Arrow Trail today. Tourism now flourishes in the entire region surrounding Mount Monadnock, which is considered the second most-climbed mountain in the world, after Japan's Mount Fuji.

While Monadnock draws the crowds, it was the region's lesser-known peaks and forest trails that drew our attention while researching this book. Time and time again we were amazed as we came across small family cemeteries or the foundations for old schoolhouses miles from the nearest road. While we were intrigued by this history, we were also awed by the power of nature to reclaim the land. With southern New Hampshire now home to numerous state parks and private conservation preserves, it easy to explore and enjoy the region's historical past and its wild, forested present.

3 trip highlights chart

SPORT	TRIP #	TRIP	REGION	DISTANCE	DIFFICULTY difficulty for bi*
Walking		Flat and Easy Walks	various	various	Easy
Hiking	1	Balance Rock and Pillsbury State Park	Dartmouth-Sunapee	2.0 miles up and back	Easy
Hiking	2	Bog Mountain	Dartmouth-Sunapee	2.2 miles up and back	Moderate
Hiking	3	Great Brook	Merrimack Valley	4.2 miles out and back	Easy
Hiking	4	North Pack Monadnock	Monadnock	3.2 miles up and back	Moderate
Hiking	5	Little Monadnock and Rhododendron State Park	Monadnock	4.4 miles round-trip	Strenuous
Hiking	6	Mount Pisgah	Monadnock	4.6 miles up and back	Moderate
Hiking	7	Skatutakee and Thumb Mountains	Monadnock	4.9 miles	Moderate
Hiking	8	Mount Pawtuckaway —North Peak	Merrimack Valley	6.0 miles round-trip	Moderate
Hiking	9	Pierce Reservation	Monadnock	6.4 miles up and back	Moderate

ELEVATION GAIN	TIME IN HOURS	NOTES
various	various	See page 32 for a list of preserves with easy hiking trails.
500	1	An easy hike to a large glacial erratic and good views of the wilderness in Pillsbury State Park.
750	2	A short, steep climb to excellent mountain views.
200	2.5	An easy hike through scenic wildlife habitat near Pawtuckaway State Park.
950	2	A moderate climb to excellent views of the Monadnock Region.
700	2.5	An interesting woods walk through a rhododendron grove and good moose habitat.
650	2.5	A moderate hike through a beautiful hemlock forest to one of the state's best views of Mount Monadnock and the southern Green Mountains.
900	3	A moderate hike through beautiful forests to two summits with good views of the Monadnock Region.
1,000	3.5	An interesting boulder field, good wildlife habitat, and excellent views on one of the best hikes in south eastern New Hampshire.
1,000	3.5	A hike on trails and old woods road to a secluded pond and excellent views from Bacon Ledge.

trip highlights chart

SPORT	TRIP #	TRIP	REGION	DISTANCE	DIFFICULTY (aerobic difficulty for biking)
Hiking	10	Mount Kearsarge	Dartmouth-Sunapee	2.5 miles round trip	Strenuous
Hiking	11	Mount Sunapee and Lake Solitude	Dartmouth-Sunapee	6.0 miles up and back	Strenuous
Hiking	12	Eagle Cliff and Red Hill	Lakes	4.2 miles up and back	Strenuous
Hiking	13	Mount Monadnock	Monadnock	5.7 miles round trip	Strenuous
Hiking	14	Mount Cardigan	Lakes	5.6 miles round trip	Strenuous
Hiking	15	Belknap Range	Lakes	11.7 miles one-way	Strenuous

SPORT	TRIP #	TRIP	REGION	DISTANCE	DIFFICULTY (aerobic difficulty for biking)
Biking	16	Tower Hill Pond	Merrimack Valley	4.0 miles round-trip	Easy
Biking	17	Fox State Forest	Monadnock	3.4 miles round-trip	Easy
Biking	18	Mountain Road—Peterborough	Monadnock	6.0 miles out and back	Moderate

ELEVATION GAIN	TIME IN HOURS	NOTES
1,100	2.25	A short, steep climb to spectacular views from one of southern New Hampshire's highest peaks.
1,650	3.5	A strenuous hike to excellent views and a remote mountain pond.
1,650	4	A strenuous climb to spectacular views of the White Mountains and Lakes Region.
1,800	4	A cliff-side walk to the summit of one of the most-climbed mountains in the world.
1,950	4.5	A challenging hike to one of the best viewpoints in New Hampshire.
3,300	8	A strenuous peak-bagger's adventure that visits nine peaks in the Belknap Range.

TECHNICAL DIFFICULTY (biking only)	ELEVATION GAIN	TIME IN HOURS	NOTES
Easy	100	1	An easy ride around a scenic pond near Manchester with other trip possibilities nearby.
Moderate	300	1	A short, fun ride that includes a visit to a virgin hemlock forest.
Easy and Moderate	900	2	A relatively short ride on an old town road with some enjoyable downhill sections.

trip highlights chart

SPORT	TRIP #	TRIP	REGION	DISTANCE	DIFFICULTY (a◆ difficulty for bikin◆
Biking	19	Beaver Brook	Merrimack Valley	7.3 miles round-trip	Moderate
Biking	20	Pawtuckaway State Park	Merrimack Valley	8.0 miles round-trip	Moderate
Biking	21	Bear Brook State Park	Merrimack Valley	12.0 miles round-trip	Moderate
Biking	22	Pisgah State Park	Monadnock	14.2 miles round-trip	Moderate
Biking	23	Sugar River Trail	Dartmouth-Sunapee	20.0 miles out and back	Moderate
Biking	24	Newfields Rail Trail	Seacoast and Merrimack Valley	26.0 miles one-way	Moderate
Biking	25	Blue Job Mountain	Lakes	14.0 miles round-trip	Moderate
Biking	26	Plymouth Mountain	Lakes	15.0 miles round-trip	Strenuous
Biking	27	Springfield to Wilmot	Dartmouth-Sunapee	20.0 miles round-trip	Strenuous

TECHNICAL DIFFICULTY (biking only)	ELEVATION GAIN	TIME IN HOURS	NOTES
Moderate with short difficult sections	600	2	An ride through beautiful forests on old woods roads and exciting single-track.
Moderate with some difficult sections	500	2.5	An advanced intermediate ride through beautiful forests with good wildlife-watching opportunities.
Moderate with an easy alternative	800	3	A classic New Hampshire mountain bike ride on single-track and old woods roads.
Moderate	1,350	3	A beautiful half-day ride through New Hampshire's largest state park.
Easy	200	3	An easy ride on a scenic, riverside rail-trail that visits two covered bridges.
Easy	550	3	A long and easy ride across southern New Hampshire on a converted railroad bed.
Easy, Moderate, and Difficult	1,200	3	A long ride on easy country roads and challenging double-track bordered by old stone walls.
Easy to Moderate	2,400	4	A strenuous ride around Plymouth Mountain on scenic country roads and backcountry double-track.
Easy to Moderate	2,200	5	A long ride on country roads and an old logging road with good views of Mounts Cardigan and Kearsarge.

trip highlights chart

SPORT	TRIP #	TRIP	REGION
Quietwater Paddling	28	Copps Pond	Lakes
Quietwater Paddling	29	Willard Pond	Monadnock
Quietwater Paddling	30	Manning Lake	Lakes
Quietwater Paddling	31	Pillsbury State Park Ponds	Dartmouth-Sunapee
Quietwater Paddling	32	Hubbard Pond	Monadnock
Quietwater Paddling	33	Grafton Pond	Dartmouth-Sunapee
Quietwater Paddling	34	Pawtuckaway Lake	Merrimack Valley
Quietwater Paddling	35	Merrymeeting Marsh	Lakes

SPORT	TRIP #	TRIP	REGION
Sea Kayaking	36	Odiorne Salt Marsh	Seacoast
Sea Kayaking	37	Portsmouth Harbor	Seacoast
Sea Kayaking	38	Great Bay	Seacoast

DISTANCE	TIME IN HOURS	NOTES
1.5 miles round-trip	1	Turtles, frogs, ducks, and lily pads are common sights on this short, easy paddle.
2.0 miles round-trip	2	Glacial erratics line the shoreline of this pond surrounded by hills and home to loons and ospreys.
2.5 miles round-trip	1.5	A short paddle among lily pads and over crystal-clear water with good views of the Belknap Range.
2.5 miles round trip with longer options; includes 150-yard portage	2	A paddle across one pond with a portage to a second, completely secluded pond surrounded by bogs, hills, and hardwoods.
3.5 miles round-trip	2	An interesting paddle among bogs, beavers, birds, and good views of Mount Monadnock.
5.0 miles round-trip	3	A half-day paddle among pine-covered islands and wildlife-filled coves.
5.0 miles round-trip with longer options	3	Pines, loons, and mountain views on the secluded northern end of this large lake.
8.0 miles out and back	4	A twisting paddle through a marsh rich in wildlife.

DISTANCE	DIFFICULTY	TIME IN HOURS	NOTES
2.5 miles out and back	Easy	1	An easy paddle in a tidal creek surrounded by a bird-filled salt marsh.
4.5 miles round-trip	Easy	1.5	A quiet exploration of the islands and wooded shoreline between Portsmouth, New Castle, and Rye.
various round-trips	Easy to Strenuous	1 hour to all day	A paddle along wooded shorelines and marshes with excellent wildlife-watching opportunities.

trip highlights chart

SPORT	TRIP #	TRIP	REGION
Sea Kayaking	39	Rye to Portsmouth	Seacoast
Sea Kayaking	40	Squam Lake	Lakes
River Trip	41	Contoocook River	Merrimack Valley
River Trip	42	Connecticut River	Dartmouth-Sunapee
River Trip	43	Merrimack River— Franklin to Boscawen	Merrimack Valley
River Trip	44	Nissitissit River	Merrimack Valley
River Trip	45	Lamprey River	Seacoast
River Trip	46	Lower Winnipesaukee River	Lakes
River Trip	47	Sugar River	Dartmouth-Sunapee
River Trip	48	Souhegan River	Monadnock
River Trip	49	Suncook River	Lakes
River Trip	50	South Branch of the Piscataquog River	Merrimack Valley

DISTANCE	DIFFICULTY	TIME IN HOURS	NOTES
6.5 miles one-way	Moderate	2.5	A scenic paddle along the rocky New Hampshire coast.
various round trips Strenuous	Easy to to 3 days	1 hour	Classic Lakes Region paddling— loons, mountain views, and wooded islands with camping opportunities.
7.0 miles	Flat water	3.5	An easy half-day paddle through the New Hampshire countryside.
5.7/13.5 miles	Flat water	6	A flatwater paddle past farms and wooded hillsides on New England's largest river.
6.3/11.0/18.0 miles	Flat water to Class II in highwater	3	An easy summer paddle on one of New Hampshire's best-known and largest rivers.
6.5 miles	Quick water	4	An early-spring paddle through scenic forests on a narrow quickwater river.
7.0 miles	Flat water to Class II	3	A diverse paddle on the longest river on the New Hampshire seacoast.
4.5 miles	Class II	2.5	A flatwater lake paddle followed by some easy Class II that is runnable throughout the summer.
3.3 miles	Class II with one Class III drop	2.5	An exciting Class II run with one challenging Class III drop.
4.5 miles	Class II	3	One of the first Class II runs in New Hampshire to open up after winter.
5.5 miles	Class II	3	5.5 miles of playful water and great scenery.
6.5 miles	Class II	3.5	A technical Class II paddle through forests and historic New Boston.

4
hiking

HIKING HAS BEEN POPULAR IN NEW HAMPSHIRE for more than 150 years, and while most people imme-diately think of the White Mountains when they think of hiking in the state, the numerous peaks south of this range provide an excel-lent opportunity to explore new places and enjoy excellent views at the same time. Since only a few of the mountains in southern New Hampshire rise above 3,000 feet, most hikes are relatively short, although numerous trails traverse steep, rocky terrain. In addition to interesting views that range from the White Mountains to the Boston skyline, hikes in southern New Hampshire provide a look at a variety of habitat types. On the trails in this book it is possible to find nesting yellow-rumped warblers in a boreal forest, walk through a mature hemlock grove with an understory of mountain laurel, and scare up a flock of wild turkeys foraging in an oak-hickory forest. The fifteen hikes that follow are our favorites in the region.

Hiking Times

Our hiking times are based on estimates in the AMC's *Southern New Hampshire Trail Guide*, and our own experiences as average thirtysomething hikers carrying fifteen to thirty pounds of gear. As a general guideline, the *Southern New Hampshire Trail Guide* estimates thirty minutes for each 0.5 mile traveled and thirty minutes for every 1,000 feet of elevation gain. Obviously, these times can vary based on the weather, your physical fitness, and how much gear you stuff into your pack. While we think these times are useful for planning a trip, your own experiences will undoubtedly vary from ours, and you should always be prepared to spend a longer time outdoors than planned due to factors such as weather and fatigue.

Trip Ratings

Trip ratings vary in difficulty based on mileage, elevation gain, and trail conditions. Easy trips are suitable for families with kids. Still, even these hikes may have short sections of significant climbing or rough footing—New Hampshire can be a rugged place, and *easy* is a relative term. Moderate hikes entail more elevation gain than easy hikes, usually between 500 and 1,000 feet. The hikes in this chapter listed as moderate can be fun for older children who have experience hiking steep and rocky trails, and are willing to hike for more than an hour or so. Strenuous trips usually take half a day or more to complete due to the significant elevation gain involved, as well as the possibility for one or more scrambles over steep rock faces. Only hikers in good physical condition with some hiking experience should consider undertaking a strenuous trip. On page 32 is a list of "Flat and Easy Walks" that are suitable for people of all abilities who are looking for a trip without elevation gain.

Safety and Etiquette

- Select a trip that is appropriate for everyone in the group. Match the hike to the abilities of the least capable person in the group.

- Plan to be back at the trailhead before dark. Determine a turnaround time and stick to it even if you have not reached your goal for the day.

- Check the weather. While there are no extensive above-treeline sections of trail south of the White Mountains, you should be aware that the weather can change quickly and create potentially uncomfortable conditions. Lightning is a serious threat on bald summits—take shelter if you hear thunder or see thunderstorms approaching. Freezing rain, rain, and fog can make steep trails over rock ledges dangerous. Summits such as Cardigan and Monadnock are significantly higher than the valleys they surround, and can therefore be much colder and windier—bring extra clothes and rain gear to these higher peaks. Know the weather forecast before you begin your hike, monitor the sky for changing weather, and be prepared to alter your route or end your hike early. For daily weather updates, you can call the National Weather Service at 603-225-5191.

- Bring a pack with the following items:

  Water—two or more quarts per person depending on the weather and length of the trip

  Food—even for a one-hour hike, it is a good idea to bring some high-energy snacks such as nuts, dried fruit, or snack bars; bring a lunch for longer trips

  Map and compass—know how to use them!

  Extra clothing—rain gear, sweater, hat

  Flashlight

  Sunscreen

  First-aid kit

  Pocketknife

  Waterproof matches and a cigarette lighter

  Binoculars for wildlife viewing (optional)

- Choose appropriate footwear and clothing. Wear wool or synthetic hiking socks and comfortable, waterproof hiking boots that give you good traction and ankle support. Bring rain gear even in sunny weather because unexpected rain, fog, and wind are possible at any time in New Hampshire's hills. Avoid wearing cotton clothing, which absorbs sweat and rain, making for cold, damp hiking. Polypropylene, fleece, silk, and wool are all good materials for keeping moisture away from your body and keeping you warm in wet or cold conditions.

- The trails in southern New Hampshire are not always as well marked as those in popular hiking destinations such as the White Mountains or Baxter State Park. Trail signs are often inconsistent or nonexistent, and trails are not always blazed on a regular basis. We have made every effort possible to describe routes accurately, and in general the trips in this book are relatively easy to follow, but care should be taken on every trip to pay close attention to your whereabouts. Use the maps in this guide (and consider bringing a U.S. Geological Survey map as well) to keep track of your location.

In addition to practicing the Leave No Trace techniques described in this book's introduction, it is also a good idea to keep the following things in mind while hiking:

- Try not to disturb other hikers. While you may often feel alone in the wilderness, wild yelling or cell phone usage will undoubtedly upset another person's quiet backcountry experience.

- When you are out ahead of the rest of your hiking group, wait at all trail junctions. This avoids confusion and keeps people in your group from getting lost or separated.

- If you see downed wood that appears to be purposely covering a trail, it probably means the trail is closed due to overuse or hazardous conditions. If a trail is muddy, walk through the mud or on rocks, never on tree roots or plants. Having waterproof boots will keep your feet comfortable, and by staying in the center you will keep the trail from eroding into a wide "hiking highway."

By taking the above precautions, you can spend your trip focusing on the pleasures of exploring the wild places that exist in southern New Hampshire. As you work your way through the renewed forest that has grown up from former pastureland in the region, you might encounter deer and moose, hawks and owls, or red efts and green frogs. Even if you do not see these animals on every hike, you will most likely encounter signs of wildlife as you sit next to an old stone wall that has evolved from a symbol of human progress to a natural feature of the forest, and that is now home to its own share of creatures—chipmunks, squirrels, snakes, and weasels. Enjoy the many great views that you find while hiking the trips in this chapter, but remember also to take time to observe the finer points of nature along the trail.

Flat and Easy Walks

Southern New Hampshire is blessed with dozens of small parks and preserves that are wonderful places to spend an hour or more walking through forests, next to rivers, or along the coast. What follows is a short list of our favorites, but if you want to find even more places, contact The Nature Conservancy of New Hampshire, the Audubon Society of New Hampshire, and the Society for the Protection of New Hampshire Forests. (See appendix B for contact information.) These groups own a variety of properties that are open to the public for hiking. Simple trail maps are usually available at the parking area or visitor center for the following preserves.

- Beaver Brook Association, Hollis: This preserve includes 1,700 acres of forests, fields, and wetlands, which can be explored via 30 miles of trails, many of which are flat and easy old woods roads. For directions, see trip #19.

- Odiorne Point State Park and the Audubon Society of New Hampshire's Seacoast Science Center, Rye: There is a lot of variety in this 330-acre park—forests, salt marsh, ponds, World War II gun bunkers, and a few miles of frontage on the Atlantic Ocean. There are more than 3 miles of easy trails and the birding is excellent. When you feel like heading inside, you can visit the science center, which has excellent historical displays and educational programs, as well as an indoor tide pool where the kids can touch starfish, urchins, and crabs. Dogs are not allowed in the park. You can park in the parking area mentioned in trip #36 or in the main lot about a mile farther south.

- Audubon Society of New Hampshire's Loon Center, Moultonborough: Two easy woodland trails wind through 193 acres of

Hiking one of the trails at Adams Point in Durham.

forests, marshes, and streams on their way to a mile of shore-line on Lake Winnipesaukee, and a potential look at loons. The Loon Center offers a variety of education programs as well. From NH 25 in Moultonborough, onto Blake Road at the Moultonborough Central School. In 1 mile, turn right onto Lees Mills Road. The Loon Center will be on your left.

- Massabesic Audubon Center, Auburn: This preserve has miles of trails through fields and forests and along Lake Massabesic, which has one of the newest nesting pairs of ospreys in the state. You can even get a bird's-eye view of the nest from "Osprey Cam," which is broadcast in the nature center. To reach the center, take Exit 1 off NH 101 and head south on the NH 28 bypass. When you are 1.9 miles south of the traffic circle with NH 121, turn left onto Spofford Road. Take the first left onto Audubon Way and follow it to the parking lot on the left in 0.25 mile.

- Great Bay National Wildlife Refuge, Newington: The 2.0 miles of trails on this air-force-base-turned-1,000-acre-wildlife-refuge visit waterfowl ponds, old fields with wildlife-attracting apple and mulberry trees, and views overlooking Great Bay. To get there, take the Gosling Road exit off the Spaulding Turn-pike (NH 16) in Newington. Follow Gosling Road south into the Pease International Tradeport. At a T-intersection, turn right and follow signs. Pets are not permitted in the refuge.

- Adams Point Wildlife Management Area, Durham: Across Great Bay from the wildlife refuge is Adams Point, where there are a few miles of trails through fields and forests and on bluffs above the bay. This is a great place to watch for bald eagles in winter. For directions, see the directions to Adams Point in trip #38.

- The Nature Conservancy's Sheldrick Forest, Wilton: This place is not quite as flat as the others, but the hiking is still easy and takes you through a recently discovered and protected old-growth forest and a total of six natural communities. From Milford, drive west on NH 101 past Wilton Center. Turn left onto Temple Road just beyond Gary's Harvest Restaurant. After 0.3 mile, bear left to cross a bridge and then turn onto Town Farm Road. It is another 0.7 mile to the preserve entrance. Parking is in a field to the left of the road.

- Fox State Forest, Hillsboro: Trip #17 explores 3.5 miles of the trails of Fox Forest on a mountain bike, but there are several miles of trails that are easy to walk. The natural variety of the forest is superb and includes a kettle hole bog, old-growth hemlocks, and a black gum swamp. See trip #17 for directions.

For more information on short nature walks in southern New Hampshire, see AMC's *Nature Walks in Southern New Hampshire* and *Nature Walks in the New Hampshire Lakes Region.*

Balance Rock and Pillsbury State Park

Difficulty: **Easy**

Distance: **2.0 miles up and back**

Elevation Gain: **500 feet**

Estimated Time: **1 hour**

Maps: **USGS Lovewell Mountain Quadrangle**

An easy hike to a large glacial erratic and good views of the wilderness in Pillsbury State Park.

THE 8,100 ACRES that make up Pillsbury State Park in Washington were once part·of a bustling farming and lumber community known as Cherry Valley, which saw its heyday in the early nineteenth century. The area has since reverted to wild forests full of moose, loons, and black bears, and the park is now one of the best wilderness destinations in the state south of the White Mountains. The hike to Balance Rock is not the most adventurous trip in this book, but it is a perfect hike for families exploring the park or for paddlers enjoying the park's ponds (see trip #31) and looking for a short side trip. The hike is easy, although it does climb 500 feet up to a lookout on the east side of Bryant Mountain. Picnic tables and pit toilets are at the parking area.

From the parking area, follow a side road to the north past an outhouse and a couple of campsites. Then turn right and walk around a metal gate, following the dirt road uphill. In about 25 yards, turn left onto the Balance Rock Trail, which starts out as wide double-track trail in a northern hardwood forest. At 0.3 mile, turn right onto a narrow footpath that diverges from the double-track,

BALANCE ROCK AND PILLSBURY STATE PARK

which has been blocked off. The trail is unmarked, but is easy to follow as it makes a series of short climbs and descents before climbing steadily at a moderate pace. The trail makes several switchbacks through an attractive sugar maple forest, reaching an outlook over North Pond at 1.0 mile. The hills beyond the pond are traversed by the Monadnock-Sunapee Greenway and are beautiful in fall, when the sugar maples turn a fiery orange.

About 25 yards beyond the lookout is a glacial erratic known as Balance Rock, a mini-van-sized boulder dropped on the side of Bryant Mountain by a glacier during the last ice age 15,000 to 18,000 years ago. To complete the hike, turn around here and hike back down the Balance Rock Trail.

Directions

From downtown Washington, head north on NH 31. In 4.1 miles, turn right into Pillsbury State Park. The parking area is in the cul-de-sac at the end of the park road in 1.4 miles.

Also Nearby

There are several longer hiking opportunities in the park, with the most interesting being a hike up to Lucia's Lookout on the Monadnock-Sunapee Greenway. For an 8.0-mile loop, follow the Five Summers Trail (from the same parking lot as the Balance Rock Trail) up to Lucia's Lookout, then follow the Monadnock-Sunapee Greenway south to the Bear Pond Trail and take this trail right back to the Five Summers Trail. Trail maps are available at the Pillsbury State Park office.

Bog Mountain

> Difficulty: **Moderate**
>
> Distance: **2.2 miles up and back**
>
> Elevation Gain: **750 feet**
>
> Estimated Time: **2 hours**
>
> Maps: **USGS New London Quadrangle**
>
> **A short, steep climb to excellent mountain views.**

BOG MOUNTAIN IS A STOP ALONG the Sunapee-Ragged-Kearsarge Greenway, an 80-mile collection of trails that forms a loop from Newbury Harbor on Lake Sunapee around the lake and over Ragged Mountain and Mount Kearsarge. For more information about the greenway, you can visit the website of the Sunapee-Ragged-Kearsarge Greenway Coalition at www.nlrec.com/orgs/srkgc.htm. The climb up Bog Mountain is relatively short. Despite its short length, there are some steep sections that will get your heart pumping, and the views of the surrounding peaks and New Hampshire countryside are well worth the effort. No facilities are available.

The trail begins in a relatively young forest of hardwoods and spruce, alternating between level sections and short, moderate climbs. The trail is well marked with white blazes, but seems to get little use—the ground is refreshingly spongy. After passing some large white pines, the trail curls to the left and ascends a rocky ridge covered with northern red oaks. As you ascend the ridge, obstructed views to the south get increasingly better until you reach an open ledge with excellent views at 0.5 mile. In addition to views of Kearsarge, Sunapee, and Monadnock, we saw signs that coyotes travel along this ridge, trotting over granite, mica crystals, and reindeer lichen and possibly stopping to eat the blueberries that line the trail.

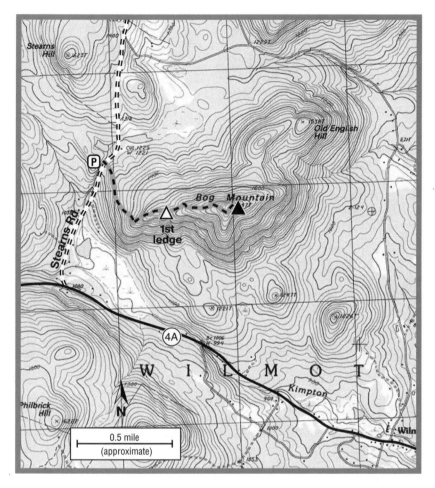

BOG MOUNTAIN

Beyond this ledge, the trail reenters the woods, climbing over more ledges populated with oaks and spruce. At 1.1 miles from Stearns Road, the trail breaks out into the open again at the base of a steep granite ledge filled with large quartz crystals. A 100-yard climb up this ledge brings you to excellent views to the south, west, and north. The actual summit is a few yards through the trees at the top of the ledge. This is the turnaround point for this trip. (The trail does continue down the east side of the mountain for about 2.3 miles to the library on North Wilmot Road.)

The view toward Mt. Cardigan from Bog Mountain.

Directions

From the intersection of NH 4A and NH 11 in Wilmot, head west on NH 4A. In 4.9 miles, turn right onto Stearns Road. The Bog Mountain Trail is on the right in another 0.8 mile, across the road and about 50 yards south of the Kimpton Brook Trail. There is limited parking on the left shoulder of the road.

Trip #3

Great Brook

Difficulty: **Easy**

Distance: **4.2 miles out and back**

Elevation Gain: **200 feet**

Estimated Time: **2¹/₂ hours**

Maps: **USGS Winchester Quadrangle**

An easy hike through scenic wildlife habitat near Pawtuckaway State Park.

THE GREAT BROOK TRAIL in Deerfield is a perfect example of how local residents can use creative means to protect wild places. The trail passes through 750 acres of forests and wetlands called the Great Brook Conservation Lands, which is actually composed of nine different parcels of land that are privately owned. The Deerfield Conservation Commission negotiated conservation easements with the owners of this land, protecting it from development and keeping it open to the public for recreation. The commission's hard work should be appreciated, because now we can all enjoy a hike through diverse wildlife habitat that is home to beavers, moose, otters, fishers, and a large variety of bird life. No facilities are available.

The Great Brook Trail traverses the 2.1 miles between Harvey Road and Coffeetown Road. You can hike it from either end or spot a car at both ends and hike it one-way. In this description, the hike starts at Harvey Road. The trail, marked with lavender paint blazes, starts in a beautiful mixed forest of beech, maple, witch hazel, pine, and hemlock. The trail climbs occasionally but is relatively easy with good footing. At 0.5 mile, you reach the top of a small bluff that overlooks a large beaver pond to views of Saddleback Mountain. In addition to beavers, the pond is home to river otters, Canada geese, and tree swallows. The trail descends to pond level

Great Brook in Deerfield.

and follows the southern shore to a side trail that leads left 150 yards to the 6-foot-tall beaver dam that holds back the waters of the pond. It is an impressive feat of rodent engineering.

Just beyond the side trail, the Great Brook Trail forks at a pair of large boulders. You can take either fork, because they join back up in about 100 yards. The left fork climbs up to look down at the marshy beginnings of Great Brook, which the trail then parallels for the next mile or so. At 1.1 miles, the trail crosses the brook on "Halfway Bridge"; there is a huge boulder on the left side of the brook and tall hemlocks on the right. You pass a small gorge on the way to a pair of brook crossings at 1.4 and 1.5 miles—in high water, these crossings can be difficult, so use caution. Hemlocks grow close to the brook where the water keeps the air cooler, while maples, birch, beech, and oaks grow in the rest of the forest, making good habitat for deer, turkey, and ruffed grouse.

At 1.7 miles, cross a small stream that flows into Great Brook. The trail continues along the waterway to the beaver pond then climbs a small hill before ending at Coffeetown Road.

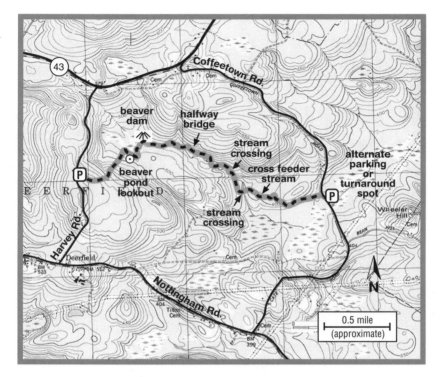

GREAT BROOK

Directions

At the northern intersection of NH 107 and NH 43, head north on NH 43. In 1.8 miles, turn right onto Harvey Road (dirt). The trailhead is on the left in 0.7 mile. Look for a green-and-white sign that says "Land Protected by Land Conservation Investment Program and Trust for NH Lands." There is room for only a few cars on the shoulder of the road.

Directions to End–of–Trail Parking

From the above trailhead, head back to NH 43 and turn right. In 0.6 mile, turn right onto Coffeetown Road. The trailhead is on the right in 1.6 miles.

Pink Lady's Slipper— New Hampshire's State Wildflower

IN 1991 NEW HAMPSHIRE named the pink lady's slipper, *Cypripedium acaule*, the official state wildflower. This orchid, which also goes by the name of moccasin flower, and blooms in late May or early June, can be found in woodlands throughout southern New Hampshire. The large, single pink (sometimes white) flower of the pink lady's slipper is $1^1/2$ to 2 inches long, is shaped like (you guessed it) a slipper, and sits atop a stalk about 12 to 15 inches tall. The flower is actually a cleverly designed trap. The bright color attracts insects, which expect a nectar reward that the lady's slipper is lacking. Instead the insect, usually a bee, fly, or beetle, is forced to follow a maze through the flower that takes it past the stamen and anthers on its way out the only exit from the flower. For lady's slippers to produce seeds, an insect must pick up pollen from the anthers of one flower and then get trapped again in a second, depositing the pollen on the stamen.

This hit-or-miss approach works, but only occasionally: lady's slippers may produce seeds only once every few years, and the event is so energy consuming that the plant often does not sprout the year following seed production. These are long-lived plants, however; they can survive for more than 100 years. Despite its long life and widespread distribution in the state, the pink lady's slipper is considered a species of special concern because it is difficult to

The pink lady's slipper is New Hampshire's official state wildflower.

propagate, it reproduces slowly, and it is vulnerable to small changes in climate. Like all orchids, pink lady's slippers require the presence of a symbiotic fungus to germinate and survive, so anything that changes this relationship will kill the plant. Other lady's slipper species found in New Hampshire are the ram's head, showy, and yellow lady's slippers. All are considered rare in the state.

North Pack Monadnock

> Difficulty: **Moderate**
>
> Distance: **3.2 miles up and back**
>
> Elevation Gain: **950 feet**
>
> Estimated Time: **2 hours**
>
> Maps: **USGS Greenfield Quadrangle**
>
> **A moderate climb to excellent views of the Monadnock Region.**

PACK MONADNOCK IN PETERBOROUGH, TEMPLE, and Greenfield has two main summits, North and South, both of which are just less than 2,300 feet tall. South Pack is part of Miller State Park and can be accessed by the park road, which leads from NH 101 to the summit. South Pack is connected to North Pack by the Wapack Trail, a 21-mile trail that starts in Ashburnham, Massachusetts, and climbs over Watatic, Barret, Kidder, and Temple Mountains on its way to the two Pack Monadnock summits. This trip starts at the northern terminus of the Wapack Trail and climbs through the Wapack National Wildlife Refuge to the undeveloped summit of North Pack Monadnock and its 360-degree views of New Hampshire and Massachusetts. No facilities are available.

From Old Mountain Road, the Wapack Trail is marked with yellow blazes, climbing moderately and then gradually through a forest of mixed hardwoods and white pines. Evergreen shrubs growing in the understory include mountain laurel, sheep laurel, and wintergreen. A layer of pine needles and a general lack of rocks in the trail make this hike easy on the feet. At 0.7 mile, the trail passes through two stone walls and then makes a short, steep climb to open ledges. These open ledges provide the occasional view north as far as Mount Washington. Scrubby oaks, pines, and spruce are growing up

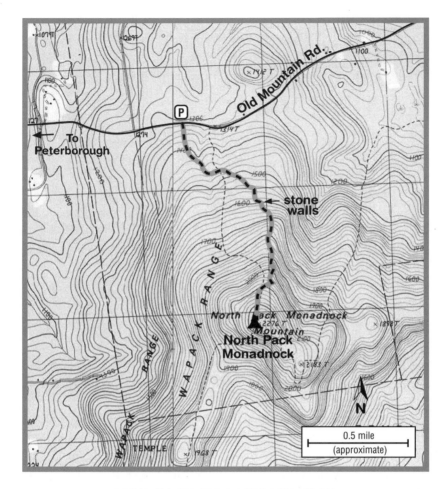

NORTH PACK MONADNOCK

around low-lying junipers, which are probably remnant shrubs from when this land was used as pasture.

At about 1.0 mile, the trail reenters the forest and alternates between steep and gradual climbing. Stone walls lining the trail give more evidence of the mountain's agricultural past. At 1.2 miles, the trail turns right and then left, climbing through a dark spruce forest for the final leg to the summit at 1.6 miles. The summit is somewhat wooded, but the surrounding ledges provide good views in all directions, particularly to the north and the west, where Mount Monadnock stands only 12 miles away. (If you are able to spot a car, you could continue on to South Pack, which is 2.6 miles and 1 1/2 hours

The Wapack Trail north of North Pack Monadnock.

to the south.) Retrace your steps to Old Mountain Road. If you are interested in hiking the entire Wapack Trail, consult the AMC's *Southern New Hampshire Trail Guide*, or contact Friends of the Wapack at P.O. Box 115, Peterborough, NH, 03468, www.wapack.org.

Directions

From the intersection of NH 101 and US 202 in Peterborough, head north on US 202 for 1.2 miles. Turn right onto Sand Hill Road. The trailhead is on the right in 4.3 miles, at which point the road's name has changed to Old Mountain Road. Park on the wide shoulder on the left.

Little Monadnock and Rhododendron State Park

> Difficulty: **Strenuous**
>
> Distance: **4.4 miles round trip**
>
> Elevation Gain: **700 feet**
>
> Estimated Time: **2$^1/_2$ hours**
>
> Maps: **USGS Monadnock Mountain Quadrangle**
>
> **An interesting woods walk through a rhododendron grove and good moose habitat.**

RHODODENDRON STATE PARK in Fitzwilliam was established in the early twentieth century to protect one of the largest rhododendron groves north of the Allegheny Mountains. There are sixteen acres of pink-blossomed rhododendrons in the park, growing 15 feet tall below large white pines and hemlock. In addition to rhododendrons, stands of mountain laurel add their own burst of color when the bloom is at its peak in mid-July. One of the best universally accessible trails in the state loops through the rhododendron grove and also visits a wildflower garden maintained by a local garden club. Please note that dogs are not allowed in the park. Facilities and picnic tables are located near the parking area.

In addition to the flower groves, the park protects more than 2,700 acres of surrounding forest, including the summit of Little Monadnock Mountain. This trip takes you through part of the rhododendron grove on its way up to Little Monadnock, and then continues over the summit and loops back to the parking area using an old woods road and Rhododendron Road.

From the parking area, walk through two granite posts and onto the Rhododendron Trail. Stay straight at a junction with the

View of Mount Monadnock from Little Monadnock Mountain.

Laurel Trail, and then turn right onto the Little Monadnock Trail 0.2 mile from the parking area. Leaving the rhododendron grove, the trail climbs moderately through a forest of maple, beech, oak, and pine, and is marked by plastic orange rectangles and white paint blazes. The many stone walls seem to be outnumbered only by acorns and beechnuts, which probably make this good habitat for white-tailed deer, black bear, and wild turkey.

The trail rolls along until it crosses a stream at 0.7 mile, where it climbs steadily to a junction with the Metacomet-Monadnock Trail (M-M Trail) and the only views of the hike at 1.1 mile. The views of nearby Mount Monadnock are excellent. Turn left onto the M-M Trail for an easy climb to the sunny but viewless summit at 1.4 miles. Continuing beyond the summit, the trail descends steadily over a narrow but well-marked footpath. The forest is dominated by white pines and red oaks; the trail is often covered with signs of moose. Like the Little Monadnock Trail, the Metacomet-Monadnock Trail passes many stone walls.

Before bottoming out, the trail winds its way through a dark hemlock grove. A lack of sunlight penetrating the thick hemlock canopy has left an understory almost devoid of plant life. After passing

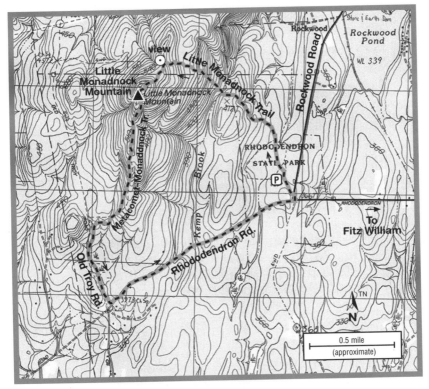

LITTLE MONADNOCK AND
RHODODENDRON STATE PARK

through the hemlocks, the trail intersects with an old town road lined with ferns and stone walls at 2.6 miles. Turn left onto this road, which is known as Old Troy Road (no car traffic). Old Troy Road passes old cellar holes and a large beaver pond on its way to Rhododendron Road at 2.9 miles. Turn left and follow Rhododendron Road (it is dirt at this point) for 1.5 miles back to the park.

Directions

From NH 12 and NH 119 in Fitzwilliam, head west on NH 119. In 0.2 mile, turn left to stay on NH 119. In another 0.7 mile, turn right onto Rhododendron Road. In another 2.1 miles, turn into Rhododendron State Park and follow the road to the hiker parking lot. There is a fee of $3 per person.

Trip #6

Mount Pisgah

> **Difficulty: Moderate**
>
> **Distance: 4.6 miles up and back**
>
> **Elevation Gain: 650 feet**
>
> **Estimated Time: 2$^{1}/_{2}$ hours**
>
> **Maps: USGS Winchester Quadrangle**
>
> **A moderate hike through a beautiful hemlock forest to one of the state's best views of Mount Monadnock and the southern Green Mountains.**

PISGAH STATE PARK, in the extreme southwestern corner of the state, is New Hampshire's largest state park: it protects more than 13,500 acres of forest, encompassing an entire watershed north of the Ashuelot River. Pisgah is a great wildlife habitat, and it is easy to explore, as there are better than 20 miles of hiking trails and another 20 miles or so of multiuse trails great for hiking or mountain biking (see trip #22). This trip to the summit of Mount Pisgah is a beautiful hike, where you will spend much of your time in a mature hemlock forest with an understory of mountain laurel. Though the main summit of Mount Pisgah is wooded and viewless, the views from the open ledges to the south are excellent. No facilities are available.

From the parking area, walk past the gate onto Kilburn Road, a narrow gravel road that is off-limits to motorized vehicles. At about 0.7 mile, you reach the first intersection with the Kilburn Loop Trail (which leads to the right for a 5.0-mile walk around Kilburn Pond). Continue straight and then turn right at 0.9 mile at the second intersection with the Kilburn Loop Trail. (An unmaintained, unmarked road goes straight.) The trail soon crosses a stream on a wooden bridge in a picturesque hemlock forest. You will make several small climbs and descents and reach the Pisgah Mountain

Crossing a bridge on the way to Mount Pisgah.

Trail at 1.2 miles. Turn left onto the Pisgah Mountain Trail, following it past a small bog and through more hemlocks with large stands of mountain laurel growing below the canopy.

At 1.6 miles, you reach the Pisgah Ridge Trail (marked with orange blazes), where you turn right and make the steady climb up to Parker's Perch at 1.8 miles. While this open ledge has the only views of the hike, they are excellent. The view of Mount Monadnock rising above the rolling countryside to the east is one of our favorite views in this entire guidebook. There are also good views west over the Connecticut River to the mountains of Vermont. If the view was your goal of this trip, you can turn around here and retrace your steps back to the parking area. If you choose to bag the wooded summit of Mount Pisgah, continue south along the Pisgah Ridge Trail, which descends into a gully before climbing to the unmarked summit at 2.3 miles.

Directions

The parking area for the Kilburn Road is on the east side of NH 63, 4.5 miles south of NH 9 in Chesterfield and 3.9 miles north of NH 119 in Hinsdale.

Also Nearby

With 20 miles of hiking trails, several hikes are possible in the park. (A complete list is available in the AMC's *Southern New Hampshire Trail Guide*. A free map published by the state park is found at the trailhead. The 1.7-mile Hubbard Hill Trail has excellent views of Vermont's Green Mountains. From NH 9 and NH 63, follow NH 63 south for 1.3 miles and turn left onto Winchester Road. The trail starts beyond a metal gate at the end of the road, 1.3 miles from NH 63.

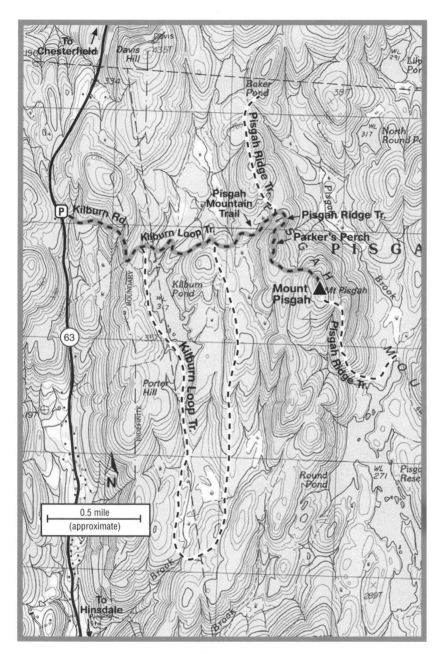

MOUNT PISGAH

Oak–Hickory and Northern Hardwood Forests

SOUTHERN NEW HAMPSHIRE is home to a variety of forest types that are found in unique habitats, including northern pine-oak forests, boreal forests, and northern swamp forests. The majority of the landscape, however, is a combination of oak-hickory and northern hardwood forest, with oak-hickory more common in the southernmost parts of the state, and northern hardwoods filling the niche between oak-hickory forests and the boreal forests farther north. Due to the extensive disturbance the landscape has experienced in the past 200 years, most forests in the region are a mixed "mosaic" forest that contains trees from several forest types. Finding a "pure" northern hardwood forest or oak-hickory forest is now more the exception than the rule.

In the northern hardwood forest the predominant trees are American beech, yellow birch, and sugar maple. The understory is populated by striped maple, a favorite food of moose, and hobblebush, with its broad round leaves and showy white flowers. Wildflowers include the pink lady's slipper, painted trillium, and wood sorrel. White-tailed deer, red squirrels, porcupines, and snowshoe hares are common in a northern hardwood forest, as are the yellow-bellied sapsucker, American redstart, black-throated blue warbler, brown creeper, and hermit thrush. The red, yellow, and orange foliage of the northern hardwood forest is responsible for northern New England's spectacular fall displays. It is also common to see trees such as white pine, northern red oak, red spruce, and paper birch filling the spaces between the three dominant tree species.

In southern New Hampshire the oak-hickory forest is dominated by oaks and hickories such as northern red oak, white oak, shagbark hickory, and butternut hickory. Common

Sugar maple leaves turn orange and yellow during New England's spectacular fall foliage displays.

in the understory are hophornbeam, mountain laurel, high-bush blueberry, sarsaparilla, and jack-in-the-pulpit. In the Northeast the oak-hickory forest was formerly called the oak-chestnut forest; American chestnut was a dominant canopy tree. In 1906, however, an invasive fungus from China was accidentally released in New York, quickly spreading and killing all American chestnut trees. While the roots of the American chestnut seem to be resistant, the sprouts that result seldom grow more than 20 feet tall before dying. In some places sugar maple has begun to replace the chestnut as a canopy tree, giving the oak-hickory more of a northern hardwoods look. Because this forest produces large quantities of nuts, gray squirrels, blue jays, and chipmunks are probably the most frequent residents. Other common animals include white-tailed deer, wild turkey, and black bear.

Skatutakee and Thumb Mountains

> Difficulty: **Moderate**
>
> Distance: **4.9 miles round–trip**
>
> Elevation Gain: **900 feet**
>
> Estimated Time: **3 hours**
>
> Maps: **USGS Marlborough Quadrangle**
>
> **A moderate hike through beautiful forests to two summits with good views of the Monadnock Region.**

HANCOCK IS HOME TO the Harris Center for Conservation Education, which provides environmental education programs to more than 4,000 students in twenty-seven Monadnock Region schools. While much of this instruction is in the classroom, there are also field studies that take place in a local "supersanctuary"—7,000 acres of protected wild forest owned by the Harris Center, The Nature Conservancy, the Society for Protection of New Hampshire Forests, and local landowners. The supersanctuary is home to several miles of trails that give access to mountain streams, remote ponds, and the summits of Skatutakee and Thumb Mountains. These two peaks, which top out at about 2,000 feet and have good views of the Monadnock Region, are the focus of this trip. Check out the Harris Center before or after your hike—it offers great programs for adults as well as kids. (You can also reach the center at 341 King's Highway, Hancock, NH 03449, 603-525-3394.) Restrooms are located within the center.

This hike loops up over Skatutakee on its way to Thumb Mountain, using the Harriskat, Thumbs Up, and Thumbs Down

Mount Monadnock from the summit of Skatutakee Mountain.

Trails. To start the hike, walk out of the parking area, following the dirt road for about 100 yards, where you turn right, following triangular Harris Center signs through the woods and back to the King's Highway.

Turn right and follow the road for about 50 yards to the trailhead on the left. Follow the Harriskat Trail, which is marked with white plastic rectangles. The trail climbs gradually, then moderately through a northern hardwood forest with scattered white pines and red oaks. At 0.2 mile, the trail makes a sharp right; then at 0.6 mile, it reaches a trail junction with the Thumbs Down Trail. Turn left to stay on the Harriskat Trail, which climbs to a flat area in a spruce forest with a beautiful understory of tall ferns.

After this flat area, the trail once again climbs moderately, then steeply past a stone wall and over a granite ledge to the open summit of Skatutakee Mountain at 1.6 miles. The summit is covered in blueberries, creeping junipers, and short oaks and provides excellent views to the south and east, including Mount Monadnock, which is only 8 miles away. To continue on to Thumb Mountain, follow the blue arrows south (down and to the right as you face the

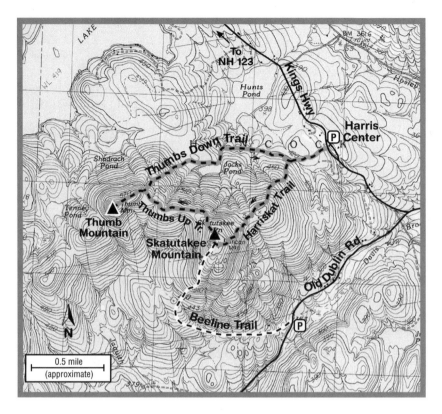

SKATUTAKEE AND THUMB MOUNTAINS

summit cairn from the Harriskat Trail). In about 40 yards, turn right onto the Thumbs Up Trail, which is marked by white plastic triangles. (The Beeline Trail, marked with blue blazes, leads 1.5 miles to Old Dublin Road.) The Thumbs Up Trail descends moderately to a level area between the peaks that is covered in another forest of ferns and spruce. The trail is sometimes narrow and somewhat obscure, but can easily be followed over the level ridge to a junction with the Thumbs Down Trail at 2.6 miles.

Turn left to make the steepest climb of the hike up to the somewhat wooded summit of Thumb Mountain at 2.9 miles, where scattered ledges provide good views of Monadnock, the Wapack Range, and the extensive forests that fill the valleys of the Monadnock Region. Very few signs of civilization are visible, which seems remarkable considering this area was heavily converted to pasture for sheep farming in the early nineteenth century. To complete the loop, take the Thumbs Up Trail back down to its junction with the Thumbs Down Trail and continue straight, following the yellow blazes. The stone walls you pass on the way once fenced in sheep pastures, but now they are in the middle of spruce and hardwood forests that are home to ruffed grouse, moose, and flying squirrels.

At 3.8 miles, you pass Jack's Pond, a secluded, undeveloped pond surrounded by hardwoods and tall white pines. Near the east end of the pond, the trail turns left following an old woods road and crossing the pond's outlet stream. At 4.2 miles, the trail turns right off the road and continues past another brook to the junction with the Harriskat Trail at 4.3 miles. Turn left to follow the Harriskat Trail back to the King's Highway and the parking area.

Directions

From the intersection of NH 137 and NH 123, head north on NH 123. In 2.2 miles, turn left onto Hunt's Pond Road. In another 0.5 mile, turn left onto King's Highway. In another 0.6 mile, turn left into parking for the Harris Center for Conservation Education.

Mount Pawtuckaway— North Peak

> **Difficulty: Moderate**
>
> Distance: **6 miles round-trip**
>
> Elevation Gain: **1,000 feet**
>
> Estimated Time: **3^1/$_2$ hours**
>
> Maps: **USGS Mount Pawtuckaway Quadrangle**
>
> **An interesting boulder field, good wildlife habitat, and excellent views on one of the best hikes in southeastern New Hampshire.**

AT A LITTLE MORE THAN 1,000 FEET TALL, Mount Pawtuckaway would receive little notice if it were in a place like the White Mountains, but in the relatively flat lands of southeastern New Hampshire, it stands tall above the surrounding woods and farms. There are actually three separate peaks on Pawtuckaway—North, Middle, and South—all the remnants of one of the last volcanic, mountain-building periods in New Hampshire, which took place around 130 million years ago. This trip visits the North Peak, which is the tallest of the three and features excellent views from several open ledges. The hike also passes Round Pond, a couple of beaver ponds, and a unique boulder field that is popular with rock climbers. Part of Pawtuckaway State Park, Mount Pawtuckaway is near several other hikes, as well as good mountain biking (see trip #20), paddling (see trip #34), and camping (see appendix D for Pawtuckaway State Park information). Please note that dogs are not allowed in the park. No facilities are available at the trailhead.

From the parking area, walk past the metal gate for 0.8 mile down a dirt road to Round Pond, a scenic pond surrounded by tall

Forest and ponds as seen from Mount Pawtuckaway.

white pines and northern hardwoods. At the pond, turn right and follow a trail that parallels a small brook as it climbs past giant boulders to a beaver pond. Standing in the water are the silver trunks of dead trees, which provide convenient perches for a variety of birds. There is also a good view across the pond to the north peak of Mount Pawtuckaway. Walking through the first of several hemlock groves you will encounter on this trip, you soon reach a trail junction; turn left, following the sign for the Lower Slab Trail. At 1.3 miles, you pass through a stone wall and reach a junction with the Boulders Trail. You will be using this trail on the return part of the loop, but for now turn right onto the North Mountain Trail.

This trail meanders through some of the nicest forest in the park, including hemlocks, white pines, and hickories. Just a few hundred yards beyond the Boulders Trail, there is a trail junction marked by a double white blaze—stay to the right and follow the trail to the shoreline of a marsh that is part of Dead Pond. The trail turns left and ascends steeply next to Devil's Den, a cliff filled with deep caves. Climb over the top of Devil's Den; at 1.8 miles, a side trail leads a few yards left to a ledge with good views to the south and east as far as the Atlantic Ocean. Beyond this side trail, the North Mountain Trail makes a short descent before climbing a series of switchbacks through a beautiful grove of mature hemlocks to another open ledge that has the best views of the hike (as well as a Public Service of New Hampshire—PSNH—communications dish).

The views from this ledge just 0.2 mile below the summit are excellent and stretch from the Atlantic in the east to Mount Monadnock in the west. In addition to the PSNH dish, the ledge is populated by creeping juniper, low-bush blueberry, small oak, and red columbine. The trail heads west behind the PSNH dish and makes a short, moderate climb to the wooded north summit of Mount Pawtuckaway at 2.2 miles from the parking area. After the summit, the trail makes a gradual descent on a ridge of open oak forest with occasional views to the Middle and South Peaks of Pawtuckaway. The trail eventually leaves the views behind and descends steeply to an intersection with a wide snowmobile trail at 3.1 miles. Turn left, following the sign for Round Pond, on what is the North Mountain By-Pass Trail.

The hike now turns into a mostly flat woods walk on a wide trail through a mature forest of beech, oak, and hemlock trees. Wildflowers such as rose twisted stalk and red trillium can be found in the understory. At about 3.6 miles, turn left as the North Moutain By-Pass Trail narrows, following a yellow arrow. The trail makes a short climb to a marshy area with good views of the mountain. Shortly after this view, make a left, following a white arrow. This trail soon ends at Round Pond Road at 4.2 miles. Turn left for a short walk to the Boulders Trail, where you turn left again.

The Boulders Trail makes its way through an area known as the Boulders, where there is a sizable collection of large glacial erratics, some 30 feet tall or more. These stones are popular with rock climbers and are fun to explore even for nonclimbers. At 4.7 miles, you reach the trail junction with the North Mountain Trail. Continue straight to return to Round Pond, where you turn left onto the dirt road to make your way back to the parking area.

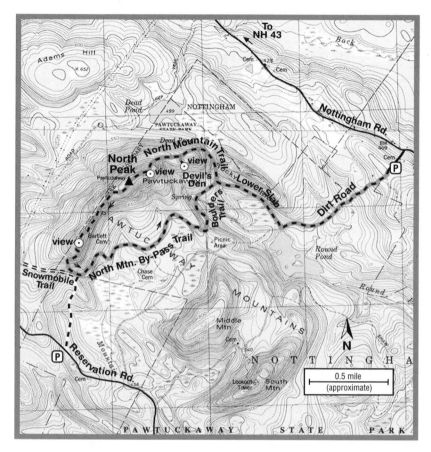

MOUNT PAWTUCKAWAY—NORTH PEAK

Directions

From the northern intersection of NH 107 and NH 43, head south on NH 43/NH 107 for 0.9 mile and turn left onto Nottingham Road. In 4.3 miles, turn right onto a dirt road that heads uphill to a small parking area in another 0.3 mile. There is room for only a few cars. Do not park on the side of the road if the lot is filled—you will get a $50 ticket. Instead, park on the shoulder of Nottingham Road and walk the extra 0.3 mile.

Pierce Reservation

> Difficulty: **Moderate**
>
> Distance: **6.4 miles up and back**
>
> Elevation Gain: **1,000 feet**
>
> Estimated Time: **3¹/₂ hours**
>
> Maps: **USGS Stoddard Quadrangle**
>
> **A hike on trails and old woods roads to a secluded pond and excellent views from Bacon Ledge.**

THE SOCIETY FOR THE PROTECTION of New Hampshire Forests (SPNHF) played a key role in the creation of the White Mountain National Forest in the early twentieth century, and it continues to protect land throughout the state today. It currently holds conservation easements on 68,000 acres of land, and owns more than 32,000 acres in SPNHF preserves. Almost 3,500 acres in size, the Pierce Reservation in Stoddard is the SPNHF's largest preserve, and it makes a great place to spend the day hiking and soaking in the views from Bacon Ledge. For more information about the SPNHF or the preserve, you can contact 603-224-9945, www.spnhf.org. No facilities are available.

Follow the grassy woods road (no motor vehicles are allowed) from the parking area as it makes a short climb before descending about 300 feet to a beaver pond and the junction with the Crescent Pond Trail at 0.6 mile. After the beaver pond, the woods road begins to climb moderately through a beautiful, mature northern hardwood forest. At 1.6 miles, you will reach a junction where another woods road leads to the right. Turn right and follow this narrow road for about 150 yards to a backcountry horse camp. Continue straight for another 100 yards to the spot where a spur path leads about 20 yards down to Trout Pond, a quiet, secluded

Taking in the views from Bacon Ledge.

pond surrounded by lichen-covered rocks, blueberry bushes, and low-lying hills.

After making the detour to the pond, follow the spur path back up to the woods road, cross the road, and follow the path to the camp. To the left of the camp is a sign for Bacon Ledge. Follow the path through a small clearing and into the woods, where there is a sign for Barrett Pond Road. The trail, known as the Trout'n'Bacon Trail, is marked with yellow wooden triangles and yellow paint blazes. It is easy to follow, though it can be somewhat overgrown in late summer and fall—wear long pants. The trail climbs gradually and, at 2.4 miles, crosses a stone wall, where a ski trail leads to the right. Continue straight as the trail levels off and winds its way around the flat and wooded summit of Round Mountain.

Once past the summit of Round Mountain, the trail drops about 50 feet, crosses a stone wall, and passes through an overgrown pasture before entering a stately old spruce forest with an understory of ferns and mosses. After the spruce grove, the trail makes another short descent, crosses another stone wall, and then reaches a trail

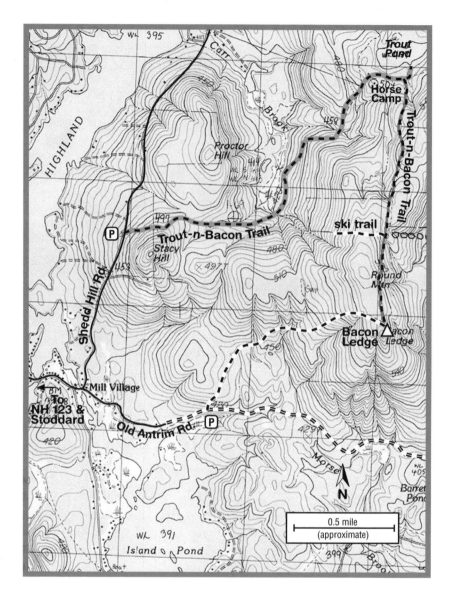

PIERCE RESERVATION

junction where the Bacon Ledge By-Pass forks to the right. Take the left fork, following the sign for Bacon Ledge. From the junction it is a short climb to Bacon Ledge, which has excellent views, especially to the east and west. We suggest making this the turnaround point of your hike. (It is possible to make a loop by continuing over Bacon

Ledge on the Trout'n'Bacon Trail for 1.1 miles to Barrett Pond Road—a.k.a. Old Antrim Road.) Take a right and follow the road for 0.8 mile to Shedd Hill Road, where you turn right and hike the pavement for an additional 0.8 mile back to the parking area.)

Directions

From the intersection of NH 9 and NH 123, head north on NH 123 for 1.9 miles, then turn left onto Shedd Hill Road. The trailhead is on the right in another 0.8 mile. Look for an old woods road blocked by a wooden gate and a Society for the Protection of New Hampshire Forests sign.

Mount Kearsarge

> **Difficulty: Strenuous**
>
> **Distance: 2.5 miles round–trip**
>
> **Elevation Gain: 1,100 feet**
>
> **Estimated Time: 2¹/₄ hours**
>
> **Maps: USGS Andover Quadrangle**
>
> **A short, steep climb to spectacular views from one of southern New Hampshire's highest peaks.**

MOUNT KEARSARGE IN WILMOT AND WARNER is one of the most conspicuous landmarks seen from I-89, its tall fire tower rising above spruce-covered slopes that peak just shy of 3,000 feet. From the somewhat isolated vantage point of the summit, there are excellent views in all directions, making Kearsarge a popular mountain to climb from either Winslow or Rollins State Parks. We will describe the hike from the Winslow State Park side, which is about twice as long as the approach from Rollins State Park, but it is still a relatively short hike that can be completed in a couple of hours. The hike makes a loop using the Wilmot Trail and the Barlow Trail—a new, scenic, and less crowded footpath.

The picnic area at the trailhead was once the site of the Winslow House, a hotel built in the nineteenth century and named for Admiral John Winslow, who commanded the USS *Kearsarge* in the Civil War. Much of the lumber used in the construction of this ship was cut from the slopes of Mount Kearsarge. The hotel was abandoned when it became unprofitable near the turn of the twentieth century, and the site was donated to the state in 1933. On the other side of the mountain, Rollins State Park was named for Governor Frank Rollins, one of the founders of the Society for the Protection of New Hampshire Forests.

Near the summit of Mount Kearsarge.

This hike makes a counterclockwise loop starting on the Winslow Trail, which is located at the east end of the parking area and marked by red paint blazes. You will start climbing immediately on a wide, well-trampled trail that passes through a spruce forest with an understory of wood ferns, bunchberries, striped maple, and an occasional mountain ash. After about 0.5 mile, the trail turns right and climbs steeply over a jumble of large rocks. The trail gets rougher and steeper as you climb, finally moderating after reaching a large boulder with good views toward Mount Sunapee and the west. Soon after this boulder, the trail breaks out onto open ledges that are sparsely populated by short spruce trees. Just below the summit, the Barlow Trail enters from the left. You reach the summit after climbing 1,100 feet and 1.1 miles.

The summit has excellent 360-degree views without climbing the fire tower. On a clear day, you can see Mount Monadnock, the Boston skyline, the White Mountains, Lake Winnipesaukee, and the mountains of Vermont and Maine. The fire tower is one of only sixteen active fire lookout towers in New Hampshire, and has been in operation since 1913, with the steel structure built in 1927 and

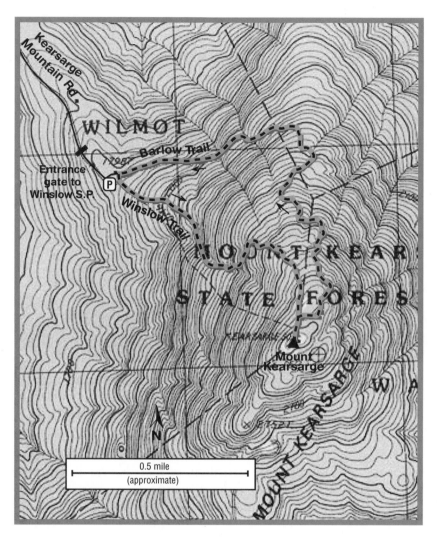

MOUNT KEARSARGE

the cab on top replaced in 2000. In addition to the fire tower, the summit is also home to an old fire warden's cabin that is no longer in use and a very large communications tower. Among all of this civilization, we found bear scat, reminding us that we were surrounded by thousands of acres of wild forest.

For the return trip, hike back down the Wilmot Trail for about 100 yards and turn right onto the Barlow Trail, which is marked by yellow paint blazes. The Barlow Trail makes a gradual descent over the rock ledges on the northeastern shoulder of the mountain. Along the way are good views of Mount Cardigan and the White Mountains. Leaving the ledges, the trail drops steeply at times, but for the most part makes a moderate descent over a trail that has more roots than rocks. About a mile below the summit, the trail almost levels off as the forest changes from spruce-fir to northern hardwoods, and then it reaches the parking area, completing the 2.5-mile loop.

Directions

Take Exit 10 off I-89 and head north, following signs for Winslow State Park. In about 100 yards, turn right at a stop sign. In about 0.5 mile, turn left onto Kearsarge Valley Road. Continue 3.1 miles and turn right onto Kearsarge Mountain Road. Follow signs for the state park, which is in another 2.2 miles. The parking area, complete with bathrooms, picnic tables, and good views, is a few hundred yards beyond the entrance. There is $2.50 fee per person.

Fire Towers

MOST OF NEW HAMPSHIRE'S sixteen active fire towers are located in the southern half of the state, and four of those are visited by hikes in this chapter—Mount Cardigan, Mount Kearsarge, Belknap Mountain, and Red Hill. With the exception of the tower on Red Hill, which is owned and operated by the town of Moultonborough, all of the towers are owned by the state and operated by the Division of Forests and Lands. All of the towers in this chapter are open to the public, and the towers on Red Hill and Belknap improve the view considerably from those mountains' mostly wooded summits. Of course, improving the view for hikers is not the purpose of the towers, which are staffed throughout the summer and fall by fire lookouts who scan the horizon for plumes of smoke.

The first fire tower built in New Hampshire was on Croydon Peak in Croydon. Built just after the turn of the twentieth century, it marked the beginning of a tower-building trend triggered by a series of fires caused by careless logging practices and sparks from the engines of logging railroad engines. Some of the first lookouts were located in existing buildings such as the hotel on Mount Moosilauke and the AMC's Madison Hut in the White Mountains. Most of the early towers were basic log buildings; the state began replacing them with steel structures in the 1920s, when there were about thirty towers in operation throughout New Hampshire.

The use of fire towers started to decline during the 1940s when the state began using airplanes to spot fires. In addition, the intense logging of the previous century had ended by this time, reducing the risk of fire. Today

The fire tower on the summit of Mount Cardigan.

airplanes still fly three fire-detection routes to augment the sixteen lookouts that remain. The tallest of these remaining towers rises 75 feet and is located on Federal Hill in Milford. Perhaps the most interesting tower in the state is the Mount Prospect tower in Lancaster, which is a unique stone structure built by U.S. Representative John Weeks in 1912. (Weeks authored the Weeks Act, which established the White Mountain National Forest in 1911.)

Mount Sunapee and Lake Solitude

> **Difficulty: Strenuous**
> **Distance: 6.0 miles up and back**
> **Elevation Gain: 1,650 feet**
> **Estimated Time: 3¹/₂ hours**
> **Maps: USGS Newport Quadrangle**
>
> **A strenuous hike to excellent views and a remote mountain pond.**

MOUNT SUNAPEE IS BEST KNOWN for its downhill ski area, which is a major landmark for those traveling north from Concord on I-89. In summer the whole Sunapee area is a popular destination for hiking, mountain biking, and boating. While the summit is overdeveloped with ski area buildings and machinery, the views are excellent in all directions. This hike up the Andrew Brook Trail on the east side of the mountain visits the summit area, but also makes a stop on the quiet, scenic shores of Lake Solitude, a small mountain pond about a mile to the east of the mass of civilization on the summit. With more than 1,600 feet of elevation gain, this is one of the more strenuous hikes in this book, but there is good footing the whole way, making it appropriate for families with hiking experience. No facilities are available at the trailhead.

From the trailhead on Mountain Road, the Andrew Brook Trail starts out as an old jeep road that climbs gradually next to Andrew Brook. This is a typical northern hardwood forest with sugar maple, beech, and yellow birch, and an understory that includes hobblebush and wildflowers such as wild oats, red trilliums, and starflowers. The trail crosses the brook often; after the third crossing

Lake Sunapee as seen from the ski slopes of Mount Sunapee.

it alternates between moderate-to-steep climbs and flat walks. At 1.3 miles, you will pass through a flat, wet area with some large yellow birch trees before the forest changes over to fir and paper birch. At 1.9 miles, you reach Lake Solitude, a beautiful mountain pond surrounded by spruce and fir and bounded on the west by the cliffs of White Ledge.

To continue on to White Ledge and then the summit, follow the trail around the northern shore of the pond to a huge yellow birch tree and an intersection with the Lake Solitude Trail at 2.0 miles. Turn right (a left here would take you to Pillsbury State Park via the Monadnock-Sunapee Greenway) and follow the trail to "Jack and June Junction" at 2.1 miles. Turn left and make a steep climb to the top of White Ledge at 2.2 miles. (A side trail leads left for about 50 yards to the top of the cliffs and excellent views to the east and north.) From White Ledge, the trail turns right and traverses a bumpy ridge in the woods until it reaches a ski area service road at 2.8 miles. Turn left onto this very steep gravel road and walk up to the summit at 3.0 miles. Scattered outlooks from around the summit

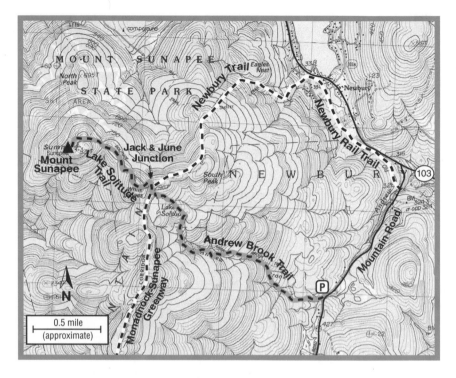

MOUNT SUNAPEE AND LAKE SOLITUDE

provide views in all directions to Mount Mondanock, the Green Mountains, and the White Mountains. Return the way you came, or follow the alternate loop route described below.

Alternate loop hike: It is possible to make a 7.0-mile loop hike by following the Newbury Trail, the Newbury Rail Trail, and Mountain Road back to the Andrew Brook trailhead. From the summit, follow the Lake Solitude Trail back down to Jack and June Junction. Go straight at this junction and follow the Newbury Trail, a narrow path marked with orange blazes. The trail starts out descending gradually, but eventually it drops down steeply, reaching a road in Newbury about 2.0 miles from the Lake Solitude Trail. Follow the road to the left into the town of Newbury, then turn right onto NH 103 and look for the Newbury Rail Trail behind a restaurant and trading post at the intersection of NH 103 and NH 103A. Follow the rail-trail south for about 1.0 mile and then turn right onto Mountain Road, which will take you back to your car.

Directions

From the intersection of NH 103 and NH 103A, head east on NH 103. In 0.8 mile, turn right onto Mountain Road. The trailhead for the Andrew Brook Trail is on the right in another 0.8 mile. Park on the wide shoulder, taking care not to block the trail.

Eagle Cliff and Red Hill

> Difficulty: **Strenuous**
>
> Distance: **4.2 miles up and back**
>
> Elevation Gain: **1,650 feet**
>
> Estimated Time: **4 hours**
>
> Maps: **USGS Center Sandwich Quadrangle**
>
> **A strenuous climb to spectacular views of the White Mountains and Lakes Region.**

RISING FROM THE EASTERN SHORE of Squam Lake in Moulton-borough, Red Hill and the fire tower at its summit are excellent vantage points for looking out over both the Lakes Region and the White Mountains. While the summit is barely higher than 2,000 feet above sea level, you will climb more than 1,650 feet in elevation on this hike, making it one of the more strenuous in this book. The steepest climb is at the beginning on the way up Eagle Cliff, an open ledge that rests 800 vertical feet above Squam Lake, only 0.5 mile away. While the Red Hill Trail on the south side of the mountain is an easier walk, the hike up and over Eagle Cliff is far more scenic. No facilities are available.

From the trailhead off Bean Road, the Eagle Cliff Trail starts climbing immediately, first moderately and then steeply as you get closer to the base of the cliff. There is some difficult scrambling over steep rocks just before reaching the open ledge at the top of the cliff at 0.6 mile, where the view of Squam Lake to the east and the Sandwich Range to the north is excellent. In summer you can feast on blueberries while taking in the views from among the scattered red and white pines and red oaks. After Eagle Cliff, the trail reenters the woods, levels off, and traverses a flat area on its way to an intersection with the Teedie Trail at 1.0 mile. (The Teedie Trail is a good

The view of New Hampshire's Lakes Region from the fire tower on Red Hill.

option for descending in wet or icy weather.) Turn left to stay on the Eagle Cliff Trail, which makes a short climb through a beautiful oak forest before descending about 100 feet to a col between Eagle Cliff and the summit of Red Hill.

The hardwood forests around Red Hill are home to big animals such as black bear and moose. The col feels wild enough for these animals to be hiding behind every tree, though you are much more likely to see smaller residents such as American toads, garter snakes, and red squirrels. From the col, the trail climbs steadily over pine needles and, about 0.25 mile below the summit, enters an area of sunny woods that were damaged by fire in 1990 and then the ice storm of 1998. About 100 yards below the fire tower, the trail intersects with the Red Hill Trail—an old fire road that comes up from Red Hill Road. Turn left for the final walk to the summit, which has excellent views of Lake Winnipesaukee to the south.

The cab atop the fire tower provides spectacular views in all directions, including the White Mountains to the north and the

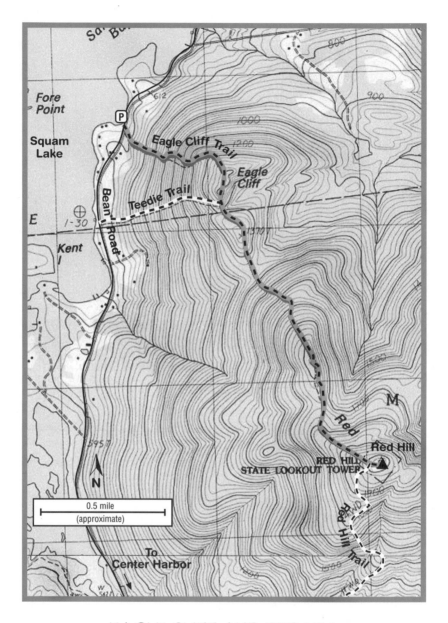

EAGLE CLIFF AND RED HILL

Lakes Region to the south. The fire tower is operated by the Moulton-borough Fire Department and has been in operation since the 1920s, when a fire tower on Mount Israel to the north was abandoned.

This is an up-and-back trip, so retrace your steps down the Red Hill Trail and take a right onto the Eagle Cliff Trail for the descent back to Bean Road.

Directions

From NH 25 in downtown Center Harbor, head north on Bean Road. The Eagle Cliff Trail is on the right in about 5.0 miles. Park on the wide shoulder on the left next to Squam Lake, about 100 yards north of the trailhead. The trailhead can be difficult to spot from the road. If you are having trouble finding it, look for the sign that says Traffic Turning—it is across the street from this sign.

Mount Monadnock

Difficulty: **Strenuous**

Distance: **5.7 miles round-trip**

Elevation Gain: **1,800 feet**

Estimated Time: **4 hours**

Maps: **AMC Mount Monadnock Map, USGS Monadnock Mountain Quadrangle**

A cliff-side walk to the summit of one of the most-climbed mountains in the world.

MOUNT MONADNOCK is one of the best-known mountains in New England. It is claimed to be the second most often climbed mountain in the world, after Mount Fuji. Visible from much of the southwestern corner of the state, the mountain is the highest point in New Hampshire south of the White Mountains, and it is also Boston's closest "big" mountain. There are 40 miles of trails on the mountain, which provide numerous options for climbing the peak. The most popular trails are the White Dot, White Cross, and White Arrow, which would best be avoided on summer and fall weekends if you are looking for solitude. Due to its length (4.5 miles one-way), the scenic Pumpelly Trail, which climbs the mountain from East Lake Road in Dublin, may be the best bet for a quiet trip during the busy season. Still, the trip described here makes an equally scenic loop from the Old Toll Road parking area, with the Cliff Walk providing a constant source of interesting views. Please note that dogs are not allowed on Monadnock's trails. Pit toilets are located at the trailhead.

From the parking area, hike up the Old Toll Road and make the moderate climb to the Parker Trail at 0.6 mile. Turn right onto the Parker Trail for a gradual descent past stone walls and northern

Mount Monadnock has been attracting visitors since the early nineteenth century.

hardwoods to the Cliff Walk at 1.0 mile, where you turn left. The Cliff Walk makes a steep 30-foot scramble over rock ledge before turning left and making its way through a flat area covered in northern red oaks. At about 1.4 miles, the trail comes to a ledge with views to the west, then soon reaches the first of several trail junctions. The Cliff Walk can be difficult to follow at times, but can be successfully navigated by looking for white C's painted on rocks and trees. Continue straight past the Hello Rock Trail and the Point Surprise Trail, both on the left. Soon after the Point Surprise Trail, you reach What Cheer Point, which has excellent views to the south and southeast.

The trail follows the contours of the cliff, moving in and out of the trees and alternating between gradual and steep climbs over sometimes rough footing. There are many blueberries as well as good views along the trail from ledges named Ainsworth's Seat, Thoreau's Seat, and Emerson's Seat for early visitors to the mountain. Stay left at an intersection with the Lost Farm Trail, continue straight at an intersection where the Thoreau Trail leads left, and stay to the right at an intersection with the Dew Drop Trail. More rough climbing brings you to an intersection with the Noble Trail and a side trail that leads to a graphite mine—stay to the right at both junctions. After 2.5 miles, you reach the end of the Cliff Walk at a small knob called Bald Rock (marked in the rock as Kiasticuticus Peak), where there are excellent views in all directions except north—the rest of the mountain blocks this view.

From Bald Rock, descend on the Smith Connecting Link by following the yellow S to the north. (Be sure not to take a left onto the Hedgehog Trail.) This trail takes you in and out of the trees on the way to the White Cross Trail 0.4 mile below the summit. Turn left and then left again in another 0.1 mile onto the White Dot Trail. From here it is a steep climb over open ledges to the summit of Monadnock at 3.4 miles. The views are spectacular in all directions: you can see the Boston skyline and Mount Washington as well as the Berkshires and Green Mountains.

Make a quick return to the Old Toll Road parking area by following the white B's north for about 25 yards and then turning left onto the White Arrow Trail, which is marked by—what else?—white arrows. It is the left-most trail, next to the cliff. The trail makes a very steep descent over rock ledges for much of the distance to the Old Halfway House site at 4.5 miles. Built in the 1850s, the White Arrow Trail is still popular today for both its scenery and its quick ascent of the mountain. Just past the Old Halfway House, you pass the Old Halfway House Trail and then the Old Toll Road. Take a

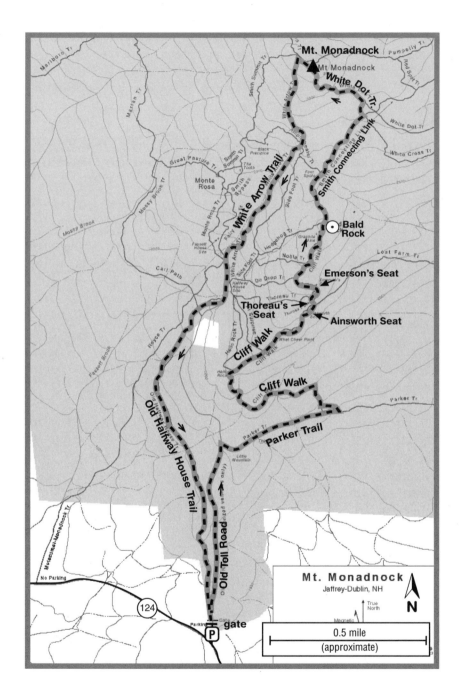

MOUNT MONADNOCK

right onto either one for the descent to the parking area at 5.7 miles. Use the trail for a more "trail-like" experience.

Directions

From the intersection of NH 124 and US 202 in Jaffrey, head west on NH 124. The parking area for the Old Toll Road and Monadnock State Park is on the right in 5.2 miles.

Grand Monadnock

AT 3,159 FEET, MOUNT MONADNOCK in Jaffrey and Dublin rises about 2,000 feet above the surrounding towns, forests, and farms, and it is the tallest peak within a radius of 40 miles. Its isolation was noted early on by geologists; indeed, *monadnock* has become the generic term for mountains that are geographically distant from other peaks. It withstood the erosion of the last ice age better than the surrounding rock because it is made of very hard metamorphic schist, much like the Presidential Range in the White Mountains. Other well-known monadnocks in New England include Mount Wachusett in Massachusetts and Mount Katahdin in Maine. Smaller mountains in the region share its name—Pack Monadnock, Gap Monadnock, Little Monadnock, and Monadnock Mountain (in northern Vermont). The mountain is officially known as Grand Monadnock to differentiate it from these other peaks.

Monadnock comes from an Abenaki Indian name that means "the unexcelled mountain." The first recorded ascent of the mountain was in 1725 by a military force led by Captain Samuel Willard of Lancaster, who along with fourteen soldiers camped on the summit during a scouting expedition. The group was looking for signs of the local Contoocook tribe, who were accused of attacking towns in the Connecticut River Valley. By the 1730s, the Contoocook had been killed or driven out of the area and colonists began to settle nearby towns. The first colonists cleared the surrounding forests for subsistence farming, but by the early 1800s the area was fully engaged in raising sheep during the wool boom.

Sheep were regularly killed by wolves, which were in turn routinely hunted and killed by local farmers. The last stronghold of *Canis lupis* in the region was the upper slopes of Mount Monadnock, and at some point before 1820 a fire was set on the mountain to drive the wolves out. This fire burned out of control, killing all of the vegetation on the

Mount Monadnock as seen from Gilson Pond.

upper slopes of the mountain. With no trees or plants to hold it in place, the thin soil soon washed off the rock, leaving the bald peak we see today. The last wolf in the region was killed during the winter of 1819-20.

With no trees to block the view, someone standing on Monadnock on a clear day can see all six New England states. Day-hikers began climbing the mountain in the 1820s, but it was not until the construction of the White Arrow Trail in

1854 and then the Mountain House in 1860 that it became a popular tourist destination. Located about halfway up the mountain, the modest Mountain House became a three-story hotel in 1866. At the southeast base of the mountain, another hotel known as the Ark became a center of activity for summer visitors. Monadnock was popular with transcendentalists; Henry David Thoreau considered it his favorite mountain. It continued to attract well-known writers into the twentieth century, including Mark Twain and Rudyard Kipling.

Painters seemed to ignore Monadnock in the early and mid-nineteenth century, instead focusing on the more "sublime" scenery of the White Mountains. They eventually discovered the beauty of the region, however, and in the late 1800s the Dublin Art Colony grew up around painters such as Abbot Thayer and Edmund Tarbell, who later became one of the best-known American impressionists. The mountain continues to inspire, and the entire Monadnock Region remains a haven for writers, artists, and composers to this day.

Today the forest on and around Monadnock is undeveloped thanks to a conservation effort that began in 1884 and led to the formation of the Monadnock Forestry Association. In 1904 the Society for the Protection of New Hampshire Forests became involved with protecting the mountain; the group now preserves more than 3,500 acres adjacent to Monadnock State Park. The park was established in 1904 and currently provides a base for hikers (and cross-country skiers in winter) with a visitor center and campground. For camping reservations or more information about the park, contact the New Hampshire State Parks at 603-271-3556.

Mount Cardigan

> Difficulty: **Strenuous**
>
> Distance: **5.6 miles round-trip**
>
> Elevation Gain: **1,950 feet**
>
> Estimated Time: **4¹/₂ hours**
>
> Maps: **AMC Mount Cardigan Map, USGS Mount Cardigan and Newfound Lake Quadrangles**
>
> **A challenging hike to one of the best viewpoints in New Hampshire.**

THE STATE OF NEW HAMPSHIRE'S website for Cardigan State Park lists hiking as the only activity in this 5,600-acre park. While backcountry skiers may argue the point, hikers are certainly grateful for the 50 miles of trails that head up and around Mount Cardigan, both in the park and in the adjacent AMC preserve. The shortest and easiest hike up Mount Cardigan (nicknamed Old Baldy) and its spectacular views is via the West Ridge Trail, which begins from the state park parking area to the west of the mountain. This trip, however, makes a loop over more interesting terrain from the east and the AMC's Cardigan Lodge, which provides overnight lodging and meals in summer and on fall weekends. Cardigan Lodge is also the setting for a variety of AMC workshops; for more information, call 603-466-2727 or surf over to www.outdoors.org. Facilities are available at the lodge.

This trip uses the Holt, Cathedral Forest, Clark, Mowglis, and Manning Trails to make the loop from the lodge up and over Cardigan and its north summit, Firescrew Mountain. With almost 2,000 feet of elevation gain, it is one of the most strenuous hikes in the book, but should pose no particular problems for hikers in reasonably good physical condition. The biggest risk is being caught on

The open ledges of Firescrew provide views to the main summit of Mount Cardigan.

the bald summit cone during bad weather, as you are completely exposed in an area prone to lightning strikes. Keep an eye on the weather and be prepared to duck quickly into the forest if the conditions deteriorate. On a good day, however, the summit of Mount Cardigan is one of the best places to be in New Hampshire, with its 360-degree views and open ridge walks.

From the parking area, walk west on the Holt Trail, which starts out as an old woods road that is a continuation of Shem Valley Road. In its first 200 yards, the trail passes the Back 80 Trail and a nature trail and then reaches the Manning Trail at 0.3 mile. Take the left fork to stay on the Holt Trail, which continues to follow an old woods road through a forest of mixed hardwoods and hemlocks, with hobblebush and striped maple in the understory. After passing a Cardigan State Park sign, the trail parallels Bailey Brook and climbs gradually until it crosses the brook and climbs moderately to Grand Junction at 1.1 miles. To follow the kinder, gentler route to the summit, turn left onto the Cathedral Forest Trail (a.k.a. Holt-Clark Cutoff). (You could, at this point, choose to continue straight on the Holt Trail for a very steep, very difficult climb to the summit—1.1 miles,

1,500 feet of elevation gain. The upper Holt Trail is not for small children or people with a fear of heights.)

In about 50 yards, take the right fork, following the sign for Cardigan Summit via Holt-Clark Cutoff. The trail climbs steadily through a mature northern hardwood forest that was probably more cathedral-like before storms destroyed much of the canopy. Despite the damage, the forest still provides cover and food for animals including moose, deer, black bear, and ruffed grouse. The trail levels off amid spruce and paper birch just prior to reaching a junction with the Clark Trail at 1.7 miles. Turn right onto the Clark Trail, which starts the final 0.9 mile to the summit with a gradual climb that gets steeper as it gains elevation. Just after passing the Alexandria Ski Trail, you reach PJ Ledge, an outlook with good views to the White Mountains. Just beyond PJ Ledge, take the right fork to stay on the Clark Trail, which works its way in and out of the trees on the way to the Fire Warden's Cabin and the South Ridge Trail at 2.4 miles.

At this point, you are at the base of the bald summit cone. Follow the trail to the right and up the very steep, smooth rock face that makes up the final 0.2 mile to the summit (follow white paint blazes). The summit sits high above the surrounding mountains, lakes, and towns. There are excellent views in every direction—the White Mountains, the Green Mountains, Mount Monadnock—and they are improved only slightly by climbing the fire tower, which was first built in 1924. The cab currently atop the tower was built in the 1960s. To the immediate north is a view of Firescrew Mountain, given its name during a forest fire in 1855 that sent flames and smoke spiraling up from its summit. The same fire cleared the upper slopes of Cardigan of all soil and vegetation.

To head toward Firescrew, walk down the Mowglis Trail (no sign) by following the white blazes that lead to the northwest (slightly to the left of Firescrew). The Mowglis Trail makes a steep descent to the col between the two summits and then follows a scenic ridge past small spruce and mountain ash, blueberries, and small wildflowers such as three-toothed cinquefoil, which blooms all summer. It is an easy, gradual climb to the summit of Firescrew (3.2 miles), where there are additional excellent views. From the top of Firescrew, take a right and follow the Manning Trail, marked with yellow blazes. The Manning Trail makes an easy traverse of the open ledges

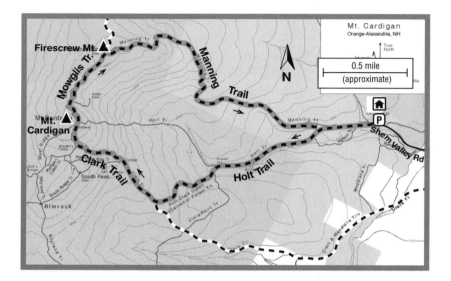

MOUNT CARDIGAN

to the east of the summit before descending steeply into the woods; this stretch can be difficult in wet or icy conditions.

After crossing a stream at about 4.4 miles, the descent moderates, and by the time the forest has changed from spruce to hardwoods, the hike has become an easy walk. At 5.3 miles, turn left onto the Holt Trail for the final 0.3 mile back to the parking area.

Directions

From the northern intersection of NH 104 and US 3A in Bristol, head north on US 3A. In another 2.1 miles, turn left in front of a stone church onto West Shore Road. In another 1.9 miles, continue straight on what is now Cardigan Mountain Road. In another 0.7 mile, bear right at a fork onto Fowler River Road. In another 3.2 miles, take the left fork onto Brook Road, following signs for the AMC's Cardigan Lodge. In another 1.1 miles, turn right onto Shem Valley Road. In 0.1 mile, bear right at a red schoolhouse. Park on the left in another 1.3 miles, across from Cardigan Lodge.

Belknap Range

> Difficulty: **Strenuous**
>
> Distance: **11.7 miles one–way**
>
> Elevation Gain: **3,300 feet**
>
> Estimated Time: **8 hours**
>
> Maps: **USGS West Alton and Laconia Quadrangles**
>
> **A strenuous peak–bagger's adventure that visits nine peaks in the Belknap Range.**

THE BELKNAP RANGE is an L-shaped string of small peaks that rise 1,800 feet to the west from the southwestern shore of Lake Winnipesaukee. At the eastern end of the range, Mount Major, with its excellent 360-degree views, is one of the most climbed mountains in southern New Hampshire. At 2,380 feet, Belknap Mountain is the tallest peak in the range, which consists of fifteen named summits above 1,500 feet. This hike is a strenuous traverse from northwest to southeast, climbing over the summits of Mount Rowe, Gunstock Mountain, Belknap Mountain, Mount Klem, Rand Mountain, West and East Quarry Mountains, Straightback Mountain, and Mount Major. The hike involves substantial elevation gain and requires good route-finding skills, because there are many trail intersections on this route, some unmarked. It is also a one-way trip, requiring the spotting of a car at either end of the range. If you are looking for a shorter hike in the range, you can hike Mount Major from the Mount Major parking area, or hike a loop up and over Rowe, Gunstock, and Belknap from the Gunstock parking area (using the Overlook Trail for the return from Belknap—see the map). No facilities are available.

This hike starts on the Ridge Trail (blazed in white), which can be found by walking north, between the Gunstock Ski Area

Lake Winnipesaukee dominates the views from the Belknap Range.

buildings and the retaining pond, past the skateboard park to a paved road on the left. Turn left onto this road which is the beginning of the Ridge Trail, marked by white blazes. After 0.3 mile and about 100 yards before you reach a ski jump, turn left onto a dirt road; when the road forks in 50 yards, bear right. This very steep dirt road soon brings you to the summit of Mount Rowe at 0.8 mile, which has some obstructed views to the north and east. Follow the white paint blazes into the woods to the left of a communications tower. The trail traverses a level, grassy ridge with good views of Lake Winnipesaukee, and then descends to the col between Rowe and Gunstock, where you bear left at the trail junction, following the white blazes. (A purple-blazed trail leads right.)

The Ridge Trail soon runs into the upper levels of the ski area, and at 1.7 miles turns right, following a ski trail and a set of water pipes. You soon come to another junction where you turn left, walk about 20 feet, and then turn right, following a white arrow and a dirt road. In another 100 yards, a double paint blaze marks the spot where the trail leaves the road and follows a ski trail on the right. Hike up this steep grassy slope for the final ascent to the summit of Gunstock at 2.4 miles, where there are buildings, ski lifts, and good views of Lake Winnipesaukee and the White Mountains.

Continue past the summit buildings to the Brook Trail and turn right, following the yellow blazes.

The quiet spruce-fir forest along the Brook Trail is a welcome contrast to all of the ski area development. At 2.6 miles, continue straight on the Saddle Trail (white blazes), where the Brook Trail turns left and descends to the Gunstock parking area. You reach another junction at the col between Belknap and Gunstock at 2.8 miles: the Overlook Trail leads left to the Gunstock parking area, and a blue-blazed trail leads right to the Belknap Carriage Road. At this point, continue straight on another blue-blazed trail that climbs the remaining 0.5 mile to the summit of Belknap Mountain, where the 34-foot-tall fire tower provides excellent views in all directions. Three summits down, six to go.

From the summit of Belknap, head south on the Old Piper Trail, following the white paint blazes. The trail descends into a clearing and, at 3.6 miles, reaches a junction. Continue south on a yellow-and-blue-blazed trail that leads to Round Pond. At 3.9 miles, take the right fork onto the Boulder Trail, which is blazed in blue. (The East Gilford Trail leads left.) The Boulder Trail descends steeply in and out of the trees with occasional views of the lakes to the south over a narrow footpath. At about the 4.0-mile mark, you cross an interesting jumble of large boulders, and at 4.2 miles, you reach an intersection with the Round Pond Link. Turn left, following the blue blazes and a sign that reads "To Gunstock and Mount Major."

At this point, you probably feel like you have left civilization far behind. The Round Pond Link rolls along through a forest of spruce and mixed hardwoods and crosses a cross-country ski trail at 4.9 miles—continue on the blue-blazed trail, following signs for Mount Major. At 5.2 miles, the trail passes an old woods road on the left and then descends a few hundred yards to Round Pond on the right. With no road access, the pond is surprisingly wild and undeveloped for the Lakes Region. It is surrounded by spruce, red pines, and boggy areas filled with blueberries, sheep laurel, and cotton grass. This scenic spot makes a good place to rest and refuel before undertaking the rest of the trip, which includes another 1,200 feet of elevation gain.

Just beyond the spot where the trail drops down to the water's edge, turn left onto the Mount Klem–Mount Mack Loop Trail, following red diamonds and making a moderate climb up and over the wooded summit of Mount Klem. The trail descends to a ledge with a good view to the north of Winnipesaukee and Mount Washington, then reaches an unmarked trail junction in an open area at 6.3 miles. Look for a cairn and white paint blazes that lead left, and follow this new trail, known as the Quarry Trail, for an up-and-down hike to Rand, West Quarry, and East Quarry Mountains. The trail is narrow and sometimes steep, but it is easy to follow as it is very well marked. There are several ledges with good views along the way; you also pass several signs of former settlements, including numerous stone walls, an old town road at 7.2 miles, and an old quarry site (marked by a cairn made of pink granite) dating from the mid-1800s at 7.4 miles.

After the quarry site, the trail makes a steep ascent over some mossy ledges that can be dangerous in wet or icy conditions—as of fall 2001, there is a safer alternate route (a detour around the ledges) marked with yellow flagging tape. Beyond East Quarry Mountain, the trail descends to a gully then makes a short, steep climb up to the northern summit of Straightback Mountain at 9.0 miles. Just beyond this summit, the trail descends to a ledge with views to nearby Mount Major. At this ledge, the trail forks. Take the left fork, which reaches the Major-Straightback Link at 9.3 miles. Turn left here, following blue blazes, for the final 0.8-mile climb to the summit of Mount Major. (Stay straight at intersections with the Brook Trail and Beaver Pond Trail.) The final 0.3 mile of this climb is over semi-open ledges populated by spruce, white pines, and blueberries.

The summit of Mount Major has excellent views in all directions, especially of nearby Lake Winnipesaukee and the distant White Mountains. To reach the Mount Major parking area, walk past the remnants of a stone hut to the Mount Major Trail (blazed in blue), which makes a very steep descent for about 0.7 mile. (This descent can be very difficult in bad weather. For a safer alternate route down, follow the Major-Straightback Link west for 0.4 mile to the Brook Trail, where you turn right and continue down to the Mount Major Trail and the parking area.) The Mount Major Trail reaches the parking area 1.5 miles below the summit and 11.7 miles from the Gunstock parking area.

BELKNAP RANGE

0.5 mile
(approximate)

N

Mt. Major

Mt. Major Tr.

Brook Trail

Major-Straightback Link

Mt. Major Link

Mt. Straightback

East Quarry Mountain

West Quarry Mountain

old quarry site

Logging Rd.

Quarry Trail

Rand Mountain

Mt. Klem-Mt. Mack Tr.

Mt. Klem

Mt. Mack

Mack Loop Tr.

Mt. Klem

Round Pond Tr.

Round Pond

Round Pond Link

Old Piper Trail

Belknap Mountain

boulder field

Boulder Trail

Green Tr.

Overlook Tr.

Brook Trail

Ski trail

Saddle Trail

Gunstock Mt.

Ridge Trail

Mt. Row

BELKNAP MOUNTAINS

BELKNAP STATE FOREST

Directions

This is a one-way hike that assumes you spot a car at the Mount Major trailhead before proceeding to the Ridge Trail at the Gunstock Ski Area. From the northern intersection of NH 11 and NH 11D, head west on NH 11. The parking area for the Mount Major Trail is on the left in 1.8 miles. To get to Gunstock, turn left out of the Mount Major parking lot and continue west on NH 11. In 2.4 miles, turn left onto NH 11A. In another 4.4 miles, turn left into the Gunstock Ski Area. Park in the lot at the end of the entrance road.

5

mountain biking

AS MOUNTAIN BIKING GAINED IN POPULARITY
during the 1990s, people discovered that southern
New Hampshire is full of great rides. The gently rolling terrain combined with a seemingly inexhaustible supply of old town and farm
roads makes the area ripe for fat tires. The state of New Hampshire
has actively promoted the use of mountain bikes in state parks and
forests, where these old roads have turned into rocky double-track
trails that wind their way through thick woods. Most of the trips in
this chapter use one or more of these "new" trails, usually in con-
junction with dirt roads and/or single-track. There are also several
easy-to-ride rail-trails in the state, two of which are described in this
chapter.

Trip Times

The times listed for the bike rides in this chapter are fairly conser-
vative and based on what we feel it would take a rider in average
physical condition to complete the trip. We do assume that you have
been riding a bike recently and that your heart and leg muscles are

in riding shape. Infrequent bikers may need more time; those who ride consistently from week to week will probably need less. You should add extra time when trails are wet or when rain is expected.

Trip Ratings

We list two ratings for each trip: aerobic difficulty and technical difficulty. Aerobic difficulty is based on the amount of elevation change and the number of miles. Trips with few ups and downs are generally listed as easy, though longer-mileage trips on gently rolling terrain may be listed as moderate. Moderate trips usually contain a fair amount of elevation gain, but in most cases it is broken up into shorter sections of climbing. On a strenuous trip, expect significant elevation gain via either steep climbs or long drawn-out climbs. Technically, an easy trip usually means that most of the riding is on a dirt road with an easily ridable surface. Moderate trips include single-tracks (narrow trails, usually hiking trails) or double-tracks (usually old town roads or snowmobile trails) that have varying amounts of roots and rocks, and require some maneuvering on the part of the bicyclist. Most intermediate riders can handle these trails. A trip rated as technically difficult usually involves a consistently difficult ride over roots and rocks, often on steep terrain. All but the best riders will end up walking sections of these trails.

Set a Good Example

In some hiking circles, mountain biking is still seen as a reckless sport that erodes trails and endangers walkers. In southern New Hampshire, however, most bike trips follow logging roads or old town roads; bicycle erosion is not a problem. Also, hikers rarely use these roads, so the incidence of hiker-biker conflict is low. Still, some of these trips do use hiking trails or intersect with hiking trails where biking is prohibited. For this reason, it is important that all mountain bikers use good judgment when riding in order to protect the environment and allow others to enjoy their wilderness experience. To practice responsible riding, follow the "Rules of the Trail" as suggested by the International Mountain Biking Association (www.imba.com):

• **Ride on open trails only.** Respect trail and road closures (ask if uncertain); avoid trespassing on private land; obtain permits or other authorization as may be required. Federal and state wilderness areas are closed to cycling. The way you ride will influence trail management decisions and policies.

• **Leave no trace.** Be sensitive to the dirt beneath you. Recognize different types of soils and trail construction; practice low-impact cycling. Wet and muddy trails are more vulnerable to damage. When the trailbed is soft, consider other riding options. This also means staying on existing trails and not creating new ones. Do not cut switchbacks. Be sure to pack out at least as much as you pack in. (Also follow the Leave No Trace guidelines set forth in chapter 1.)

• **Control your bicycle.** Inattention for even a second can cause problems. Obey all bicycle speed regulations and recommendations.

• **Always yield trail.** Let your fellow trail users know you are coming. A friendly greeting or bell is considerate and works well; do not startle others. Show your respect when passing by slowing to a walking pace or even stopping. Anticipate other trail users around corners or in blind spots. Yielding means slowing down, establishing communication, and being prepared to stop if necessary and pass safely.

• **Never scare animals.** All animals are startled by an unannounced approach, a sudden movement, or a loud noise. This can be dangerous for you, others, and the animals. Give animals extra room and time to adjust to you. Use special care when passing horses and follow directions from the horseback riders (ask if uncertain). Running cattle and disturbing wildlife is a serious offense. Leave gates as you found them, or as marked.

• **Plan ahead.** Know your equipment, your ability, and the area in which you are riding—and prepare accordingly. Be self-sufficient at all times, keep your equipment in good repair, and carry necessary supplies for changes in weather or other conditions. A well-executed trip is a satisfaction to you and not a burden to others. Always wear a helmet and appropriate safety gear.

Most trail erosion in New Hampshire occurs during spring and after heavy rains. Try to avoid riding on single-track trails at these times. In southern parts of the state, trails are pretty muddy from the time the snow melts until at least June. We usually wait until July anyway, to avoid the hordes of black flies.

Safety and Comfort

Because all of the bike trips in this book explore terrain at lower elevations, bad weather is more likely to cause discomfort than serious danger. Of course, rain and wet leaves can make descending on rocky trails a more dangerous proposition, and long rides on a cold, rainy day can create hypothermic conditions. Most mountain biking accidents occur on technical trails, where riders get going too fast for their abilities. For a safe and comfortable mountain biking experience, keep your bike under control at all times and consider the following tips:

- Select a trip that is appropriate for everyone in the group. Match the ride to the abilities of the least capable person in the group.

- Plan to be back at the trailhead before dark. Determine a turnaround time and stick to it even if you have not reached your goal for the day.

- Check the weather forecast. Avoid riding during or immediately after heavy rains. Give yourself more time to stop in the rain— wet brakes do not work as well as dry ones.

- Bring a pack or pannier with the following items:

  Water—two or more quarts per person, depending on the weather and length of the trip

  Food—even for a one-hour trip, it is a good idea to bring some high-energy snacks such as nuts, dried fruit, or snack bars; bring a lunch for longer trips

  Map and compass, and the ability to use them

  Extra clothing—rain gear, sweater, hat

Flashlight

Sunscreen

First-aid kit

Pocketknife

Basic bike maintenance tools and a spare inner tube and/or tire repair kit

- Wear appropriate footwear and clothing. Consider wearing hiking boots or mountain biking shoes, because having to push or carry your bike over rough trails is a real possibility. Legwear should be tight fitting. Loose pants can get stuck on pedals and in the gears of a bike, causing nasty accidents. Bring rain gear even in sunny weather: unexpected rain, fog, and wind is possible at any time in New Hampshire's mountains. Avoid wearing cotton clothing, which absorbs sweat and rain, making for cold, damp riding. Polypropylene, fleece, silk, and wool are all good materials for keeping moisture away from your body and keeping you warm in wet or cold conditions.

- In general, the bike trails in southern New Hampshire are not marked very well, if at all. Trails are usually wide and easy to follow, but unmarked intersections are common, and it can be difficult to determine when you have reached the intersection you are looking for. We have made every effort possible to describe routes accurately, but care should be taken on every trip to pay close attention to your whereabouts. Use a compass and the maps in this guide (and consider bringing a U.S. Geological Survey map as well) to keep track of your location.

The trips in this chapter range from an easy, flat ride along the banks of the scenic Sugar River to thigh-burning climbs around Plymouth Mountain and exhilarating single-track descents near Beaver Brook. You will experience the rewards of exploring the New Hampshire countryside as well as penetrating deep into the biggest forests south of the White Mountains. (If lift-served downhill riding is your pleasure, you will want to visit the Gunstock Ski Area in Gilford, which has miles of varied terrain and is open from Memorial Day weekend through Columbus Day weekend. For more information, call 800-GUNSTOCK or visit www.gunstock.com.)

Tower Hill Pond

> **Aerobic Difficulty: Easy**
>
> **Technical Difficulty: Easy**
>
> **Distance: 4 miles round-trip**
>
> **Elevation Gain: 100 feet**
>
> **Estimated Time: 1 hour**
>
> **Maps: USGS Candia and Manchester North Quadrangles**
>
> **An easy ride around a scenic pond near Manchester with other trip possibilities nearby.**

THIS LOOP AROUND TOWER HILL POND is an easy trip that makes a great warm-up or after-work ride. The pond is a reservoir that is part of the Lake Massabesic watershed, which provides drinking water for about 125,000 people in the Manchester area. (Swimming is not allowed). Facilities are not available.

To start this trip, ride past the metal gate onto Snowmobile Trail 15. It is a very rough first 200 yards that you might need to walk, but the rest of the trip is on an easy dirt road surface. The trail follows Tower Hill Pond's outlet stream until it reaches a dam at 0.5 mile. Turn left at the dam and then bear right at a fork in about 100 yards. There is a short, steep climb up to the top of the dam, where you get your first look at the 157-acre pond, surrounded by oaks and white pines. Follow the road in a clockwise direction, staying left at a fork in another 100 yards. There are occasional side trails leading off into the woods on the left or down to the pond on the right. At **2.4 miles**, you pass Snowmobile Trail 15 and cross the inlet to the pond on a bridge. At **3.5 miles**, you return to the top of

Mountain biker over the dam at Tower Hill Pond.

the dam. Continue straight and then turn right in about 50 yards. When you reach the base of the dam, turn left to return to the car.

Directions

From NH 101, take Exit 2 and head south. About 0.2 mile south of NH 101, take the first left. In another 0.5 mile, turn left onto Tower Hill Road. Park on the shoulder in about 100 yards. The trail is past a metal gate on the left side of the road.

Also Nearby

In addition to this 4.0-mile loop, you can also explore some of the short but fun single-track trails that branch off from this main loop. Though we have not tried it, fit and adventurous riders can supposedly follow Snowmobile Trail 15 from the north end of the pond for 10 miles to Bear Brook State Park and ride the trails there as well (see trip #21). You can also make this a longer trip by parking at Lake Massabesic and following the Newfields Recreation Trail for 3.7 miles to Snowmobile Trail 15, then take this north for

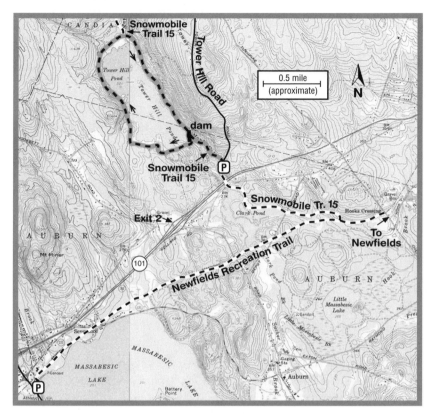

TOWER HILL POND

1.2 miles to the beginning of this trip. (See trip #24 for directions.) There are also single-track trails south of Tower Hill Pond off Snowmobile Trail 15; they are maintained by FOMBA, Friends of Massabesic Bicycling Association. For more information, check out www.fomba.com, or write to FOMBA, 69 Appletree Road, Auburn, NH 03032.

Trip #17

Fox State Forest

> Aerobic Difficulty: **Easy**
> Technical Difficulty: **Moderate**
> Distance: **3.4 miles round–trip**
> Elevation Gain: **300 feet**
> Estimated Time: **1 hour**
> Maps: **USGS Hillsboro Upper Village Quadrangle**
>
> **A short, fun ride that includes a visit to a virgin hemlock forest.**

FOX STATE FOREST IN HILLSBORO protects almost 1,500 acres of forest that includes 22 miles of trails for hiking and biking. The forest is comprised mainly of northern hardwoods, oaks, and white pines, but there is also a stand of 450-year-old black gum trees and a grove of virgin hemlocks. This short loop is perfect for a quick early-morning or late-afternoon ride. It visits the virgin hemlock grove as well as an interesting bog where a 21-foot-thick mat of peat is topped with carnivorous pitcher plants. Along the way you might see wild turkeys, great horned or barred owls, hawks, or white-tailed deer. If you have time to explore other parts of the forest, you can pick up a trail map at Fox headquarters and spend a few hours exploring all the nooks and crannies in the area. Highlights include Hurricane Road, the Black Gum Swamp, and Monroe Hill Tower with its views of Crotched Mountain and Mount Monadnock. There are bathrooms in the headquarters building.

To start this loop, ride out of the parking lot and take a right onto Center Road. In about 100 yards, turn right onto Concord End Road—a dirt road that rolls gently past stone walls, a cellar hole, and an old family cemetery. At **0.7 mile**, turn right onto Gould Pond Road, an old town road that is now an easy-to-ride double-track that

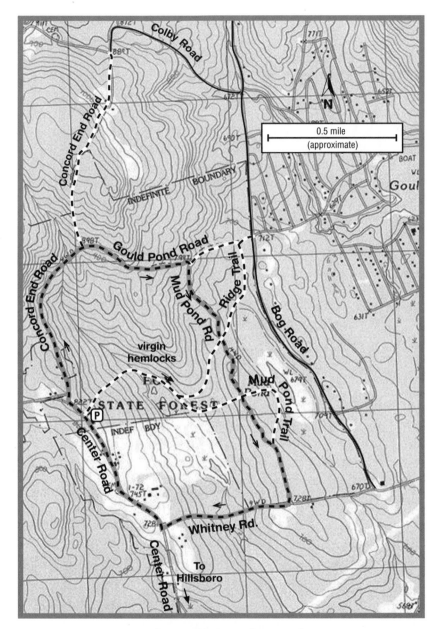

FOX STATE FOREST

passes more stone walls and cellar holes marking the locations of abandoned barns and farmhouses. At **1.2 miles**, you pass the Gould Pond Trail on the right, which heads back to park headquarters.

Continue straight on Gould Pond Road for another 50 yards, then turn right onto Mud Pond Road. Except for a few water bars in the first 100 yards, Mud Pond Road is an easy double-track trail. At **1.4 miles,** the Ridge Trail comes in from the left, and then leaves to the right at **1.6 miles.** To visit the virgin hemlock forest, stash your bike here and walk on the Ridge Trail for about 0.25 mile to an enchanting grove of old-growth hemlocks and American beech trees, some of which are estimated to be more than 400 years old.

Once you are back on Mud Pond Road, ride another 0.2 mile to the Mud Pond Trail and stash the bike again. Take a left onto the Mud Pond Trail and walk the 100 yards down to a boardwalk that provides access to Mud Pond Bog. Travel without the boardwalk would be difficult, since the sphagnum moss is more than 20 feet deep in spots! This nutrient-poor environment still manages to support a variety of plants—larch trees, blueberries, sheep laurel, cotton grass, and pitcher plants, which get their nutrients by trapping insects in their sticky leaves. The pond and bog were created about 15,000 years ago when a chunk of glacier broke off and settled here, eventually melting and creating what is known as a kettle hole. The pond is also a great place to watch for birds such as ducks, swallows, kingbirds, and hawks.

To finish the trip, walk back to your bike, then continue riding south on Mud Pond Road to Whitney Road at **2.3 miles.** Turn right for a 30-yard ride on pavement and then continue straight as Whitney Road turns into a moderately technical double-track that leads you past more stone walls and a beaver pond on its way to Center Road at **2.8 miles.** Turn right onto Center Road for a beautiful ride past farms back to the park headquarters at **3.4 miles.**

Directions

From the western intersection of US 202 and NH 9, head east on US 202. In 1.4 miles, you reach a light in the center of Hillsboro. Turn left onto School Street, which becomes Center Road. The parking area for Fox State Forest is on the right next to the forest headquarters building, 2.0 miles from US 202.

Eastern Hemlock—
Under Attack

THE GRACEFUL, DARK GREEN EASTERN HEMLOCK,
Tsuga canadensis, can be found throughout New Hampshire
from sea level to about 3,000 feet. Hemlocks are shade-
tolerant trees that have a unique requirement for cool,
moist air. Because of this need, hemlock stands most often
occur along streams in ravines where cool air settles, and
on the cooler, wetter northeastern slopes of hills and
mountains. Filling this ecological niche, they range from
Cape Breton Island in Atlantic Canada south to the mountains in northern Alabama, and they occur in a wide variety of forests including boreal, northern hardwood,
Appalachian Cove, and more. They are evergreens with
cinnamon-brown bark; short, flat needles about $1/2$ inch
long are shiny dark green above and a duller green with
two white bands underneath. Living 500 years or more,
eastern hemlocks can grow to be impressive trees, up to
80 feet tall and 3 feet in diameter.

The hemlock woolly adelgid is thought to have been
accidentally introduced to the United States from Asia in
1924. The small, aphidlike insect has since destroyed thousands of acres of both eastern and Carolina hemlocks from
the Smoky Mountains in North Carolina to southern New
England. By sucking the sap from the new twigs, the
insects prevent a tree from growing; the tree eventually
loses its needles and dies within a few years. The loss of
hemlocks in eastern forests can have a serious impact on
stream ecology, because the light-tight canopy of a hemlock forest plays a major role in moderating water temperatures. Hemlocks also provide cover for many bird species

A grove of virgin hemlock trees in Fox State Forest.

and are preferred by ruby-crowned kinglets as nesting habitat.

Some insecticides can control the woolly adelgid, but their widespread use is impractical because of the negative impact on riparian habitats where hemlocks are common. Scientists are currently experimenting with natural predator controls, including ladybird beetles and insects from the Southwest and Pacific Northwest. The woolly adelgid has yet to establish itself in New Hampshire, but it is present in neighboring Massachusetts. If you are in a New Hampshire hemlock forest, take a quick look at the new twigs on the trees. If you spot white, woolly egg masses on the undersides of these twigs, the tree may be infested. Contact the New Hampshire Forest Health Program managed by the New Hampshire Division of Forests and Lands at 603-271-7858 (www.nhdfl.com). We can, hopefully, all help stop the spread of these insects that threaten one of our most majestic trees.

Mountain Road— Peterborough

> **Aerobic Difficulty: Moderate**
> **Technical Difficulty: Easy and Moderate**
> **Distance: 6.0 miles out and back**
> **Elevation Gain: 900 feet**
> **Estimated Time: 2 hours**
> **Maps: USGS Peterborough South Quadrangle**
>
> **A relatively short ride on an old town road with some enjoyable downhill sections.**

MOUNTAIN ROAD IN PETERBOROUGH is an old town road that travels through the forest between NH 123 in Sharon and Cunningham Pond in Peterborough on NH 101. The first half of the road is dirt, and still used by local residents, while the second half is moderately technical double-track. Mountain Road travels up and over a small hill to the west of Temple Mountain, eventually running into Condy Road just before reaching NH 101. There are good views near the end of the road as you pass farms and a pond. While this is not really a destination trip, if you are in the Peterborough area and looking for a quick, scenic bike ride it is a perfect option.

From the parking area, follow Mountain Road north as it rolls along over an easy-to-ride dirt surface. You pass through typical southwestern New Hampshire scenery: fields bordered by stone walls and a forest of mixed hardwoods, white pines, and hemlocks. At **1.5 miles,** you pass a house on the left with a wooden fence next to several sugar maple trees. Just beyond this house, you will need to ride around a metal gate—the road beyond this point is off-limits

A quiet pond in Peterborough.

to cars. The road begins to climb, sometimes steeply, over moderately technical terrain, soon becoming a double-track trail lined on both sides by stone walls and majestic oak trees. After cresting the hill, you get to make a fun descent over grassy double-track on the way to another metal gate at **2.4 miles.**

Just beyond this gate, turn right and follow a dirt road that passes through a farm bordered by wooden fences. You pass a few houses and then a scenic pond on the right, which provides excellent views of Pack Monadnock. Now on Condy Road, you reach NH 101 at **3.0 miles.** To return to your car, just turn around and retrace your tire tracks.

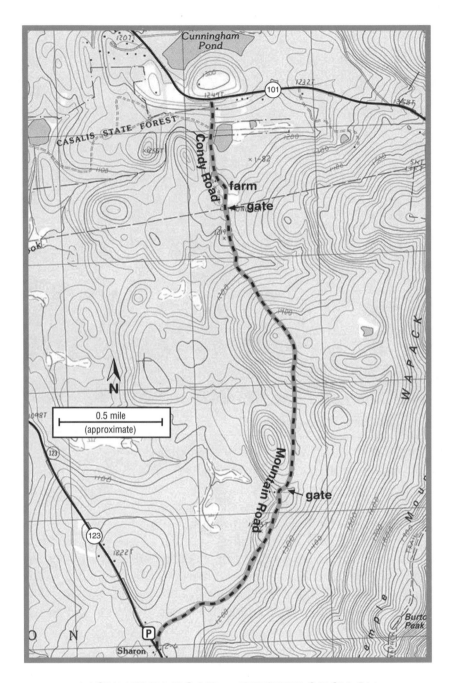

MOUNTAIN ROAD—PETERBOROUGH

Directions

At the southern intersection of NH 101 and NH 123 in Peterborough, head south on NH 123. Mountain Road is on the left in 3.9 miles, across from the Sharon Arts Center. Park next to Mountain Road in the parking lot for the Three Maples Inn (a bed-and-breakfast if you need a place to stay in the Peterborough area: 603-924-3503). The owner kindly allows bikers to use his lot, so please be respectful of his private property.

Beaver Brook

Aerobic Difficulty: Moderate

Technical Difficulty: Moderate with short difficult sections

Distance: 7.3 miles round-trip

Elevation Gain: 600 feet

Estimated Time: 2 hours

Maps: USGS Pepperell (Massachusetts) and Townsend (Massachusetts) Quadrangles

A ride through beautiful forests on old woods roads and exciting single-track.

BEAVER BROOK IS A SMALL STREAM in Hollis that flows into the Nissitissit River near the Massachusetts border. The Beaver Brook Association has protected nearly 2,000 acres of land around Beaver Brook that offers opportunities for hiking, skiing, horseback riding, and mountain biking. This trip explores a little more than 7 miles of trails that pass through a variety of forest types and visit a wildlife pond that is an excellent spot for bird watching. It uses old woods roads and some of the most enjoyable single-track you will find in this book. While there are some advanced technical sections, they are short enough that less-skilled riders can walk them and still have a fun ride. The Beaver Brook Association manages its trails for multiple uses, but some (marked with yellow triangles) are for hiking only—stay on the trails marked with blue squares. All of the trails are well marked, and detailed trail maps are available at the office near the parking area. Pit toilets are available at the trailhead.

To start this trip, ride down the old woods road (Cow Lane) that heads north from the parking lot. This is an easy ride over a smooth **dirt** surface through a beautiful forest of white pines and

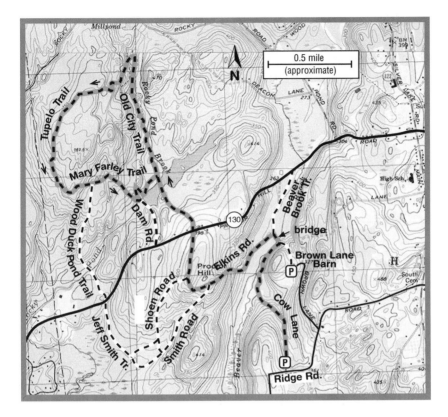

BEAVER BROOK

oaks with a few hemlocks and mountain laurel as well. At **0.8 mile**, turn left onto the Beaver Brook Trail, which leads over a bridge to Elkins Road, where you turn left again. Elkins Road is a moderately technical climb on a single-track trail. (You will have the pleasure of descending this trail on the return part of the trip.)

At **1.3 miles**, take the right fork at a junction with Smith Road to stay on Elkins Road. At **1.5 miles**, you will come to a T-intersection; turn right onto Old City Trail (unmarked), which leads to NH 130.

At **1.8 miles**, cross NH 130 and follow the trail past a barn back into the forest. At **2.2 miles**, cross the beaver pond on a wooden bridge. There is a good view of a beaver dam from the bridge, and the pond is an excellent place to look for ducks and great blue herons. Just beyond the bridge, continue straight at an intersection with the Mary Farley Trail. After the pond, the trail gets rougher, but there is a reward: a ride through a beautiful hemlock forest and walls of mountain laurel. At **3.1 miles,** turn left onto the Tupelo Trail for a ride on some excellent single-track. The trail climbs over moderately technical terrain as it skirts a tupelo swamp on the left. Black tupelo, also known as black gum, is a tall tree (up to 100 feet) whose juicy blue-black berries are favorites of birds and other animals. In fall the glossy leaves of tupelo trees turn a brilliant scarlet.

After passing the swamp, the Tupelo Trail becomes increasingly more technically difficult and will challenge most riders, forcing some to walk their bikes. At **4.4 miles,** you reach an intersection with the Wood Duck Pond Trail on the right—continue left on what is now the Mary Farley Trail (unmarked). Enjoy the fun downhill single-track to **4.8 miles,** where you will reach a pond and the Jeff Smith Trail. Stay to the left to remain on the Mary Farley Trail and follow it back to the Old City Trail at **5.0 miles.** Turn right and retrace your route to the parking area using the Old City Trail, Elkins Road, and Cow Lane.

Directions

At the intersection of NH 130 and NH 122 in Hollis, head south on NH 122. In 0.9 mile, turn right onto Ridge Road. In 1.1 miles, turn right into the parking area for the Maple Hill Farm office of the Beaver Brook Association.

Pawtuckaway State Park

> **Aerobic Difficulty: Moderate**
>
> **Technical Difficulty: Moderate with some difficult sections**
>
> **Distance: 8.0 miles round-trip**
>
> **Elevation Gain: 500 feet**
>
> **Estimated Time: 2¹/₂ hours**
>
> **Maps: USGS Mount Pawtuckaway Quadrangle**
>
> **An advanced intermediate ride through beautiful forests with good wildlife-watching opportunities.**

PAWTUCKAWAY STATE PARK, with its lake, beach, and 15 miles of trails, is one of the most popular parks in New Hampshire. Mountain bikers have been riding the park's trails for years because of their scenic variety and single-track challenges. This 8.0-mile trip has some easy riding, but for the most part it takes you over technical single- and double-track that requires some skillful maneuvering. Experienced riders on rigid forks will have no problem with this trip, but they may feel a little beat up by the end due to long stretches of rocky trail. Thankfully, there are many places to take a break on this ride as it passes scenic ponds and streams, and tunnels its way through beautiful hardwood forests. Please note that dogs are not permitted in the park. Restrooms are available at the visitor center near the park entrance.

From the Mountain Trail trailhead, ride northeast on the paved park road for **1.0 mile,** where you turn left onto the Fundy Trail. In about 50 yards, take the left fork to continue on the Fundy Trail, which passes a wildlife-rich boggy area at **1.5 miles.** This sphagnum bog, filled with blueberry bushes, rushes, and dead

Wooden bridges help with the stream crossings in the hardwood forests of Pawtuckaway.

standing tree trunks, is excellent habitat for insect- and berry-eating warblers, swallows, and flycatchers, as well as hawks and kestrels. The trail is relatively level with a few small ups and downs. It is also a pretty easy trail, although there are some bumpy spots. At **1.9 miles,** pass a side trail on the right; at **2.0 miles,** cross a stream on a wooden bridge and come to a T-intersection with a big 4 painted on a white pine. (You can take a right to continue on the Fundy Trail for another 0.5 mile, where you reach the boat ramp at Fundy Cove on the lake.) For this trip, turn left to follow the Shaw Trail. There is no trail sign, but the path is marked with white blazes.

At **2.4 miles,** the trail crosses a wooden bridge over a stream between two beaver ponds. There is a good look at a beaver dam on the right. This is also another good place to scan for birds and even moose. Beyond this bridge, the Shaw Trail is a rocky and rough but enjoyable single-track experience—except in spring, when the beavers make travel difficult by flooding the trail in spots. Try the ride in fall, when there are myriad colors on the birches, oaks,

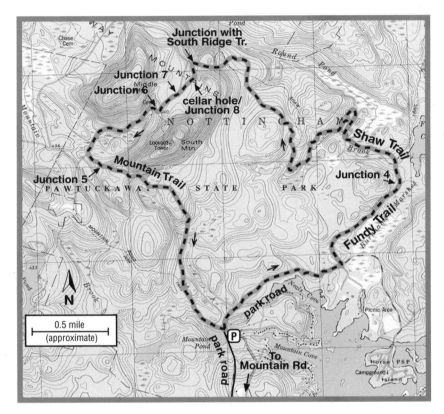

PAWTUCKAWAY STATE PARK

maples, and hickories. Beyond the beaver pond, the trail is moderately technical on its way to a pair of Winnebago-sized rocks covered in rock tripe lichen at **3.3 miles.** After crossing a stream at **4.3 miles,** the trail gets very technical, climbing steeply at times over rocky terrain. At **4.8 miles,** the trail crosses a stream in a small, picturesque gully filled with large sugar maples and white pines. (At this point, the South Ridge Trail leads to the right for a difficult 0.5-mile side trip to Round Pond and the Boulders Trail.)

Continue on the Shaw Trail as it makes a left and a short climb to an old cellar hole near a tree marked with a big 8. At **5.1 miles,** turn left onto a dirt road (Tower Road) at Junction 7. At **5.3 miles,** a hiking trail on the left leads 0.4 mile to the fire tower on the south peak of Mount Pawtuckaway. Continue on the road, which bears right beyond the trail. At **6.0 miles,** turn left onto the Mountain Trail (no sign) about 50 yards before the end of Tower Road. In about 100 yards, stay right at the fork, and then stay right again at the fork at Junction 5. At **6.6 miles,** there is an unmarked trail on the left—continue straight. The Mountain Trail is fun moderate-to-advanced riding, with the downhills providing numerous endover possibilities. At **7.5 miles,** reach a T-intersection and turn left onto a former town road that provides an easy downhill ride all the way to the end of the trip at **8.0 miles.**

Directions

From the intersection of NH 107 and NH 156 in Raymond, head north on NH 156. In 1.4 miles, turn left onto Mountain Road. In another 2.0 miles, turn left into Pawtuckaway State Park. In another 0.5 mile, park on the shoulder at the north end of Mountain Pond, across the road from the Mountain Trail. If there is no room here, you can park in the lot at the park entrance and bike the 0.5 mile to the trailhead. There is a $3-per-person day-use fee.

Endangered Species in New Hampshire

DESPITE THE FACT THAT MUCH of New Hampshire's forests have returned and most of its rivers have been cleaned up, there are many animals that the state considers endangered or threatened with extirpation from the state. There are twenty-four animals on the state's endangered list, including the Canada lynx and timber rattlesnake, and

A piping plover returns to New Hampshire's beaches.

twelve on its threatened list, including such popular species as ospreys and common loons. Seven of the state's endangered animals are also listed as federally endangered or threatened species: Canada lynx, bald eagle, piping plover, roseate tern, shortnose sturgeon, dwarf wedge mussel, and Karner blue butterfly.

The New Hampshire Fish and Game Department has a Nongame and Endangered Wildlife Program that works to protect these animals through monitoring, research, education, and outreach. Recent programs have included a plover monitoring project at Seabrook and Hampton Beaches that resulted in the first successful piping plover nests in New Hampshire since the mid-1970s and a tern recovery project on two of the Isles of Shoals. One of these islands now hosts the second largest common tern colony in the Gulf of Maine.

A project proving more difficult is an effort to help New Hampshire's state butterfly, the Karner blue—a small, attractive violet-blue butterfly with a wingspan of about 1 inch. The New Hampshire population, which is less than 100, lives on only one site in Concord, and is separated from the main populations of the butterfly in eastern New York and the Mid-

Chicks from this piping plover nest in Seabrook were the first to fledge in New Hampshire in more than twenty years.

west. The state is working with the New Hampshire chapter of The Nature Conservancy to improve habitat in the Concord pine barrens that support wild lupine, the species' only food source. They are using prescribed burns and planting wild lupine as well as introducing Karner blue eggs collected from the New York populations. Development and fire suppression have greatly reduced the acreage of New Hampshire's pine barrens, which in turn has reduced the number of Karner blues and other insects. While we are lucky to have such large tracts of wilderness in the northern part of the state, the plight of the Karner blue butterfly highlights the need to conserve smaller tracts of habitat in the south as well. Efforts such as this one are necessary to save unique plant and animal species and provide wild corridors that animals can use to travel between the larger wild places in New England. For more information about endangered species in New Hampshire, visit the websites of the Nature Conservancy and Audubon Society (see appendix B) and the website of New Hampshire Fish and Game, www.wildlife.state.nh.us.

Trip #21

Bear Brook State Park

> **Aerobic Difficulty: Moderate**
> **Technical Difficulty: Moderate with an easy alternative**
> **Distance: 12 miles round-trip**
> **Elevation Gain: 800 feet**
> **Estimated Time: 3 hours**
> **Maps: USGS Suncook, Gossville, Manchester North, and Candia Quadrangles**
>
> **A classic New Hampshire mountain bike ride on single-track and old woods roads.**

WITH MORE THAN 40 MILES OF TRAILS, Bear Brook State Park in Allenstown is one of the best places to ride in New Hampshire. It is also one of the biggest parks in the state—more than 8,000 acres—providing a large stretch of wilderness relatively close to Concord and Manchester. In addition to biking, the park offers hiking, camping, swimming, fishing, and archery. There are trails at all levels of difficulty in the park; you could easily spend a few days exploring all of them. This trip follows mostly rocky intermediate terrain, but there are also some easy sections, including a 4.5-mile loop that can be ridden as a separate trip. Except for one short foray outside the park boundary, this trip has a wild feel as you pass through many forest types and visit an old reservoir held back by a historic rock dam. Please note that dogs are not allowed on the trails in Bear Brook.

From the parking area, which has pit toilets, turn right onto Podunk Road, and in another few yards take a right at the fork. Podunk soon changes from pavement to an easy-to-ride dirt road that reaches Snowmobile Trail 15 on the right at **0.8 mile.** (This

An old reservoir in Bear Brook State Park.

connects Bear Brook to trips #16 and #24.) At **0.9 mile**, you pass the Chipmunk Trail and XC9—this trail will be part of an easy loop at the end of this ride. At **1.1 miles**, reach Junction D, turn right onto the Hedgehog Ledge Trail, and ride the gentle downhill over rocky double-track past the Ferret Trail to Junction B at **1.8 miles.** Turn right onto the Lowland Trail, which starts as a technically challenging, level ride through a wet area before turning into smooth single-track that takes you downhill to Junction A at **2.4 miles.** Turn left onto an old woods road that soon leaves the park. This old town road starts as rolling, moderately technical single-track, but eventually turns into a long downhill ride over double-track that passes a couple of private roads (stay left at both intersections) on its way to a metal gate at **3.9 miles.**

At the metal gate, turn left onto a dirt road (Dodge Road), and at **4.1 miles,** follow the road to the left, avoiding the entrance to a gravel pit. You are now on a narrow, unmaintained dirt road surrounded by private property—please stay on the trail during this short section outside the park. You reenter the park at **4.3 miles** and,

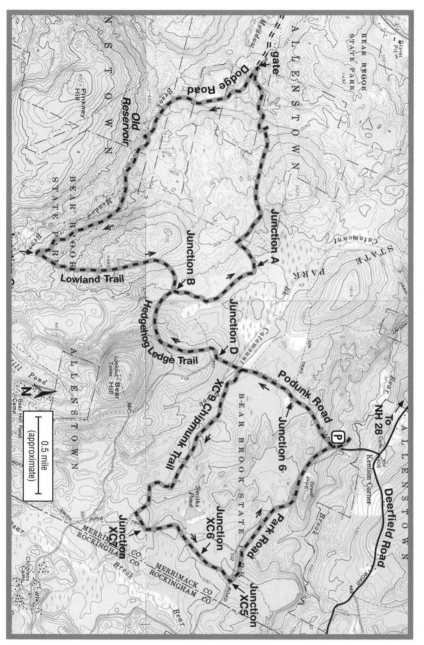

at **4.8 miles,** reach a scenic old reservoir, which makes a great place for a lunch break. The reservoir is held back by a stone dam made of large granite blocks. The dam is now breached in the middle with a large red maple tree growing in its center. Below the dam, Boat Meadow Brook cascades over rock ledges bordered by dark green hemlocks.

Beyond the dam, the road turns to the left and follows the shore of the reservoir and the brook. Beavers have been hard at work, which means that depending on the season and the year, parts of this road can be very wet and even flooded. At **5.2 miles,** an unmarked trail comes in from the right—continue straight. The road is now a moderately technical double-track that rolls along before finishing with an enjoyable 0.2-mile stretch of single-track ending at Junction C, **6.0 miles** from the start of the trip. Turn left at Junction C onto the Lowland Trail, heading back toward Podunk Road. The Lowland Trail provides more moderately technical terrain through a forest of white pines and mixed hardwoods—oaks, maples, and beeches. Much of the park has a similar forest makeup, which provides good food for wild turkeys, white-tailed deer, and a variety of small mammals. At **7.7 miles,** turn right at Junction B onto the Hedgehog Ledge Trail.

At **8.4 miles,** you return to Junction D and Podunk Road; turn left. At **8.6 miles,** turn right at intersection XC9. (Go straight if you prefer to skip this easy 4.5-mile loop on level single-track.) This is a fun single-track ride through tall pines on a dirt trail with few rocks. Continue straight at intersections with XC8 and XC14. At about **9.5 miles,** the trail makes a left-hand turn and then reaches intersection XC7 at **10.1 miles.** Turn left and follow this wide, pine-needle-covered trail until you reach the park road at **10.8 miles,** staying right at two forks along the way. Turn left onto the paved park road for an easy 1.2-mile ride back to the parking area.

Directions

From NH 4 and NH 28 in Epsom, head south on NH 28. In 5.7 miles, turn left onto Deerfield Road. (This road is about 3 miles north of US 3.) Drive past the main entrance to the park and then turn right onto Podunk Road, 3.1 miles from NH 28. The parking area, is on the right in another 0.3 mile.

Pisgah State Park

> Aerobic Difficulty: **Moderate**
>
> Technical Difficulty: **Moderate**
>
> Distance: **14.2 miles round–trip**
>
> Elevation Gain: **1,350 feet**
>
> Estimated Time: **3 hours**
>
> Maps: **USGS Winchester Quadrangle**
>
> **A beautiful half–day ride through New Hampshire's largest state park.**

COVERING MORE THAN 21 SQUARE MILES, Pisgah State Park is New Hampshire's largest state park, and it provides some of the best mountain biking in the entire state. The park, which lies in parts of Winchester, Chesterfield, and Hinsdale, contains beautiful stands of second-growth forests, including northern hardwood, oak-hickory, and hemlock forests. This ride is a good intermediate trip, with some moderately technical riding and many short climbs. You will ride past numerous signs of the area's settled past—stone walls, cellar holes, and cemeteries—some of which are marked by park signs. If you want to explore more areas of the park, pick up a trail map at the parking area—it outlines which trails are appropriate for bikes and which are for hiking only. Pisgah is home to moose, bear, and coyote, so keep your eyes peeled for wildlife. There are no facilities at the trailhead.

From the parking area, follow the continuation of Horseshoe Road past a metal gate. It is a fast downhill ride on gravel until you reach a fork at **0.4 mile.** Take the left fork, and then continue straight at **0.6 mile** onto Old Chesterfield Road at an intersection with Old Winchester Road. From here it is a downhill, moderately technical ride on a double-track trail as you pass several hiking trails

An old cemetery in Pisgah State Park.

and beaver ponds on the way to a parking area for the Chestnut Hill Trail at **2.1 miles.** Continue straight on the level gravel road, passing the Fullum Pond Trail at **2.3 miles,** the Nash Trail at **2.8 miles,** and the Snow Brook Trail at **3.6 miles.** Stone walls are common in this stretch. At **3.8 miles,** you come to Broad Brook Road on the right. Before continuing straight on Old Chesterfield Road, ride about 50 feet down Broad Brook Road to check out a cellar hole. This is all that remains of an old school that was used from 1835 to 1899. Standing in the middle of a mature forest, miles from any houses, it takes some imagination to picture the landscape that must have surrounded the school in the nineteenth century.

At **4.3 miles,** turn left onto Jon Hill Road, which rolls up and down over rough, broken pavement. At **5.4 miles,** you pass an unmarked ATV trail and then come to a T-intersection. Turn left and follow Old Spofford Road for 3 miles of riding outside the park boundary. This dirt road begins as an easy ride over gently rolling terrain that passes a few houses. It becomes narrower and rougher as

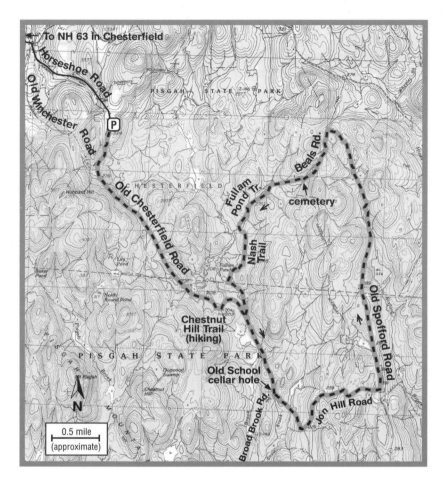

PISGAH STATE PARK

you get farther north, and at **6.3 miles,** you ride through a pair of big rocks that mark the end of the dirt road and the beginning of a double-track trail. The next 2 miles are rocky and wet, as the trail passes a series of beaver ponds that occasionally flood the trail—wear waterproof boots. While the beavers have created a rough ride for mountain bikers, they have also created some good wildlife habitat full of bullfrogs, red-spotted newts, hawks, and moose. At **8.6 miles,** there is a Pisgah State Park trailhead; turn left onto Beal's Road.

Beal's Road is a fairly rock-free double-track trail that climbs steeply over grass and weeds to the Beal's Knob Trail at **8.9 miles.**

Continue straight on Beal's Road and descend steeply over moderately technical double-track to a cemetery that dates from 1790 at **9.2 miles.** Beal's Road descends another 0.25 mile to the Fullam Pond Trail, where you turn left. From here, it is an easy downhill ride to the Nash Trail at **10.2 miles,** where you should turn left again for an enjoyable rolling ride back to Old Chesterfield Road at **11.4 miles.** Turn right onto Old Chesterfield Road and follow it, and Horseshoe Road, back to the parking area.

Directions

From the intersection of NH 9 and NH 63, head south on NH 63. In 1.1 miles, turn left onto Old Chesterfield Road. In another 0.3 mile, turn right onto Horseshoe Road. Park at the end of the road in another 1.4 miles.

Stone Walls

YOU MIGHT HAVE NOTICED that we mention stone walls a lot. The reason for this is simple—they run through the forest in almost every trip in this book. It is estimated that there are more than 100,000 miles of stone walls in New England, most of which were built during a thirty-year period between 1810 and 1840. The proliferation of stone walls in New England's forests leads people unfamiliar with New England history to suspect that they were built to mark property

A stone wall marks pasture reclaimed by forest.

boundaries. In fact, most were built to keep sheep in their pastures or out of fields with crops. Known as stone fences in the old days, walls with larger rocks were built around pastures and hay fields. Fields that were plowed for crops year after year were also surrounded with walls, but these included the smaller rocks that worked their way to the surface each spring during plowing. The walls were built by hand without mortar by the people who farmed the land. On a good day, they could build 20 feet of wall, 4.5 feet high.

Today stone walls are an important part of New England history and create a unique ecological niche in the forest. They provide hiding places for numerous animals, especially chipmunks and snakes, but are also home to a variety of insects and lichens that might not live in the forest without this artificial habitat that has now become a part of the natural landscape. If you are interested in delving deeper into the history of stone walls or you have the urge to build your own, check out *Granite Kiss* by Kevin Garder.

Sugar River Trail

Aerobic Difficulty: Moderate

Technical Difficulty: Easy

Distance: 20.0 miles out and back

Elevation Gain: 200 feet

Estimated Time: 3 hours

Maps: USGS Springfield (Vermont), Newport, and Sunapee Quadrangles

An easy ride on a scenic, riverside rail–trail that visits two covered bridges.

THE SUGAR RIVER TRAIL is a 10-mile section of the Claremont-Concord Railroad that was abandoned in 1977, then turned into a multiuse trail that parallels the scenic Sugar River as it winds its way from Newport to Claremont. The trail has very little elevation gain and we have given it a moderate rating only because the out-and-back distance is 20.0 miles, although you can spot a car in the town of Claremont if you would prefer a shorter ride. In addition to exploring the wooded shoreline of the river, the Sugar River Trail also passes through two covered railroad bridges. No facilities area available.

From the trail sign, ride north through the parking lot past a propane tank and a metal gate onto the trail—a wide dirt surface that is easy to ride on, except for the very occasional sandy spot. You make the first of several river crossings at **0.4 mile,** and then cross a road at **0.5 mile.** After this crossing you head out of Newport into quieter surroundings—forests of hardwoods, white pines, and hemlocks. At times the trail rises to 40 or 50 feet above the river, giving you a good look at the Class II rapids that are popular among paddlers in spring (see trip #47). You cross another bridge and then a

The Sugar River Trail passes through two covered railroad bridges.

road at **2.6 miles,** and then cross the river two more times in the next 0.5 mile. At **4.8 miles,** you pass under NH 11 in Kelleyville.

At **5.8 miles,** you pass through the first covered bridge. At **6.1 miles,** the trail crosses and parallels a dirt road—ride on the

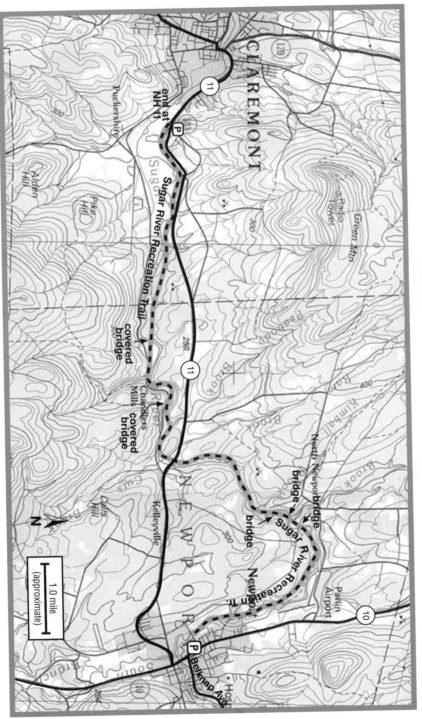

SUGAR RIVER TRAIL

road, as there are still railroad ties on this section of trail. At **6.7 miles,** the trail crosses the road again; follow the trail to the right past a metal gate. At **7.0 miles,** you pass under the second covered bridge. These are two of only five remaining historic covered railroad bridges in the entire United States. Beyond the bridges, it is a scenic ride along the river past hardwood forests, farms, and fields with views of the distant hills. The trail crosses streams at **8.3** and **9.1 miles,** and reaches a small parking area on NH 11 at **9.5 miles.** The trail continues on the side of NH 11 for another 0.5 mile until it reaches the strip malls and fast-food restaurants in Claremont.

Directions

At the southern intersection of NH 10, NH 11, and NH 103 (stoplight by Irving Station), head north on NH 10 and drive through Newport Square. In 0.5 mile, turn left onto Belknap Avenue. In another 0.1 mile, park on the right in the lot with the Sugar River Trail sign. The trail begins at the north end of the parking lot.

Newfields Rail Trail

Aerobic Difficulty: Moderate

Technical Difficulty: Easy

Distance: 26.0 miles one-way

Elevation Gain: 550 feet

Estimated Time: 3 hours

Maps: USGS Newmarket, Epping, Mount Pawtuck-away, Candia, and Manchester North Quadrangles

A long and easy ride across southern New Hampshire on a converted railroad bed.

THE NEWFIELDS RAIL TRAIL is typical rail-trail fare: easy, level riding past towns and through forests. At 26.0 miles one-way, it is a long ride, but the good riding surface means it can be completed in only three or four hours if you spot a car at each end. At times the scenery is less than appealing—you cross many roads and pass through developed areas—but you are rewarded with long stretches passing through oak-hickory forests and along lakes and beaver ponds. These wilder settings provide opportunities to spot wildlife such as great blue herons, white-tailed deer, and wild turkeys. You will also experience the less-wild excitement of riding under some of the busier roads and through metal culverts. The trip can be ridden from either end; this description takes you from Newfields to Lake Massabesic, passing a few restaurants along the way in Raymond.

From the abandoned rail station in Newfields, the trail starts out as a wide dirt road heading west. It passes backyards, farms, and beaver ponds and is flanked by stone walls for much of the way. After **7.4 miles**, you cross NH 125 in Epping and soon come to a junction with another rail-trail that leads left toward Fremont and Salem. At **11.0 miles**, you cross the Lamprey River on your way to

The Newfields Rail Trail—wide, flat, and easy.

NH 107 at **12.2 miles,** where there are fast-food pit stops in either direction. Continuing across NH 107, you cross the Lamprey again at **12.7 miles** and reach the center of Raymond at **13.2 miles.** Here you will find a couple of old train cars and the Raymond Historical Society.

At **14.5 miles,** you begin the prettiest stretch of the trip as you pass Onway Lake and ride through oak forests past deep ravines, small cliffs, beaver ponds, and a meandering stream surrounded by marsh. At **20.2 miles,** you pass through a long culvert under NH 101, and then pass Snowmobile Trail 15 at **22.7 miles.** (This connects to Tower Hill Pond; see trip #16.) At **23.5 miles,** the trail crosses a bridge over scenic Clark Pond and then passes through another culvert. Lake Massabesic is soon visible on the left. At **25.8 miles,** turn left onto a side trail that leads 0.2 mile through tall white pines to the parking area at Massabesic Lake Park.

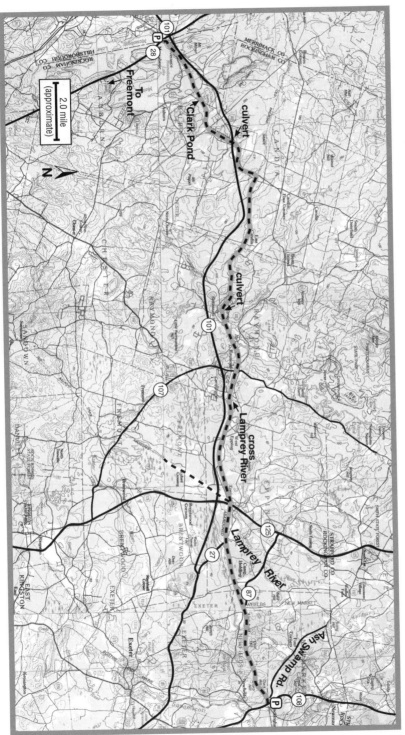

NEWFIELDS RAIL TRAIL

Directions to Newfields Parking

From NH 108 and NH 85 in Newfields, head north on NH 108. In 0.8 mile, turn left onto Ash Swamp Road (also marked as Old Route 108). In about 0.1 mile, as the road bends to the right, continue straight and park next to the abandoned train station.

Directions to Lake Massabesic Parking

From NH 101, take Exit 1 and head south on the NH 28 bypass. In 0.2 mile, continue south on NH 28 through a rotary intersection with NH 121. Just south of the rotary, turn left into the parking area at Massabesic Lake Park.

Blue Job Mountain

> **Aerobic Difficulty: Moderate**
>
> **Technical Difficulty: Easy, Moderate, and Difficult**
>
> **Distance: 14.0 miles round-trip**
>
> **Elevation Gain: 1,200 feet**
>
> **Estimated Time: 3 hours**
>
> **Maps: USGS Baxter Lake and Parker Mount Quadrangles**
>
> **A long ride on easy country roads and challenging double-track bordered by old stone walls.**

THIS RIDE MAKES A LONG CIRCUMNAVIGATION of Blue Job Mountain, one of the few peaks in southeastern New Hampshire. Most of the trip is on easy maintained dirt roads that pass through rolling countryside, but there are a few miles of riding on rocky double-track—eroded old town roads that now wind their way past stone walls and through quiet hardwood forests. You will also climb about 1,200 feet on this trip, but it is pretty easy to handle, because there are no long, sustained climbs. In addition to passing through forests, this trip will take you to beaver ponds, farms, and a bog, creating the potential to see a variety of wildlife. We saw ruffed grouse, deer, and a barred owl on our ride, and the area is also known to harbor red fox, moose, and black bear. No facilities are available.

This trip starts at the intersection of Meaderboro Road, Poor Hill Farm Road, and Reservoir Road (Cross Road on some maps) in Farmington. Start riding south on Reservoir Road. Enjoy **0.75 mile** of easy downhill past the Rochester Reservoir to Sheepboro Road, where you turn right. This starts out as a narrow dirt road with a good riding surface that rolls along through a forest of northern

Stone walls are a common sight in the area near Blue Job Mountain.

hardwoods, hemlocks, and white pines. You soon pass a beaver pond on the left. There are a few private driveways on this road, but you never see a house. At **1.6 miles**, a driveway comes in from the left—continue straight on Sheepboro Road as it becomes a narrow double-track trail that climbs over moderately technical terrain. There are stone walls along most of this road, hinting at the agricultural past of the region. At about **2.0 miles**, the trail makes a steep but short advanced technical climb over rock ledge. At **2.3 miles**, pass a red house and come to a fork, where you turn right. At **2.5 miles**, turn left at a T-intersection and continue climbing over moderately technical, rocky double-track. At about the **3.0-mile** mark, the trail gets easier and descends until it hits pavement at **3.2 miles**, where you turn right.

In about 200 yards, the road passes the trailhead for Blue Job Mountain. (It is about a thirty-minute hike to excellent views from a fire tower at the summit.) At **4.2 miles**, the road turns to dirt; at **4.7 miles**, turn right where the road forks. At **5.0 miles**, the road becomes a Class VI four-wheel-drive road—continue straight. (Class VI roads are old town roads that are no longer maintained.) This part

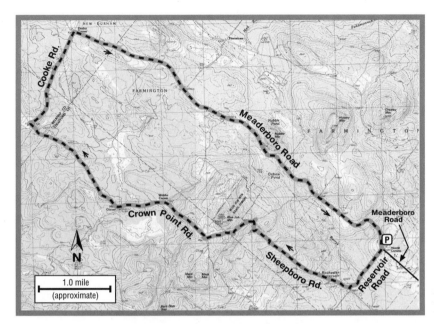

BLUE JOB MOUNTAIN

of the ride through a beautiful northern hardwood forest is moderately technical due to severe erosion from motorized vehicles, but it is a little easier than Sheepboro Road. At **6.4 miles,** the road passes a pond then makes a steep climb past a farmhouse to Cooke Road. Turn right onto Cooke Road, which has a good dirt surface, making it an easy ride to Meaderboro Road at **8.1 miles.** Turn right onto Meaderboro and follow it back to where you parked. The ride includes about 2.0 miles of downhill on pavement and a view of Blue Job Mountain from a large pond surrounded by an extensive bog. The trip finishes with a short uphill over a washboard dirt surface.

Directions

From NH 16, take exit 13 and head west on US 202. After about 1.2 miles, turn right onto Estes Road. Follow Estes Road, which becomes Meaderboro Road, for 4.3 miles to the corner of Meaderboro Road, Poor Hill Farm Road, and Reservoir Road. Park on the wide shoulder of Meaderboro Road, about 0.1 mile northwest of this intersection.

Tracking—Reading the Signs of Nature

ENCOUNTERING WILDLIFE ON A HIKE, bike ride, or paddle is always an exciting experience, but many of New Hampshire's animals are rarely seen on a typical day trip. Learning

Red fox tracks.

to read the signs that animals leave behind can open up a whole new world. You discover not only which animals have passed through a particular place, but also what those animals were doing there, what they ate, and how they interacted with other animals. Dan Gardoqui, cofounder of White Pine Programs in Dover, New Hampshire, says, "Tracking is the process of observing and interpreting phenomena in the natural world. The process of tracking helps people feel more connected to the earth and find their roots in nature." Taking the time to see and understand the signs of such animals as bobcats, otters, or coyotes is a fun and easy way to enhance any outing in New Hampshire. Tracking has of course been around for as long as humans have been hunting wildlife. Today it is also used for wildlife management, law enforcement, search and rescue, wildlife awareness, and recreation.

The actual art of tracking revolves around studying animal tracks and droppings, or scat, and other disturbances such as rubs, scrapes, digs, claw marks, and game trails. Common signs even the untrained eye can find in New Hampshire are deer and moose tracks or scat along trails, and the claw marks of bears on the trunks of beech trees. With practice, you can learn to spot where a moose spent the night, what a bear had for lunch, or the course a squirrel took in its attempt to outrun a bobcat. The easiest way to get started in tracking is to pick up a tracking field guide or how-to book such as *A Field Guide to Animal Tracks* by Olaus Murie or *Tracking and the Art of Seeing* by Paul Rezendes. Then just head out into the woods and poke around places such as ponds, riverbanks, and wet, boggy places filled with shrubs like alders. With a little practice, you will be finding animal signs on every trip you take into the wilds.

Luckily, the only way to get really good at tracking is to spend time outdoors studying nature's clues. Learning from an experienced tracker can also be a great way to accelerate the process. In New Hampshire you can take classes through White Pine Programs of Dover, New Hampshire (www.whitepineprograms.org) or through the AMC (www.outdoors.org).

Plymouth Mountain

> Aerobic Difficulty: **Strenuous**
>
> Technical Difficulty: **Easy to Moderate**
>
> Distance: **15.0 miles round–trip**
>
> Elevation Gain: **2,400 feet**
>
> Estimated Time: **4 hours**
>
> Maps: **USGS Ashland and Newfound Lake Quadrangles**
>
> **A strenuous ride around Plymouth Mountain over scenic country roads and backcountry double–track.**

THIS TRIP CIRCUMNAVIGATES PLYMOUTH MOUNTAIN on a variety of roads and trails. Pavement and dirt roads provide plenty of easy riding, and a few double-track trails add some technical challenges, while hills throughout the ride will make your thighs burn from time to time. Once you are past the Plymouth neighborhood at the start of the trip, you will generally be in a countryside setting with a couple of forays into undeveloped forests that hold a few historical surprises, including old cellar holes and a small cemetery where soldiers from the Revolutionary War are buried. With 2,400 feet of elevation gain, much of it in the backcountry, do not attempt this trip unless you are in good physical condition. No facilities are available.

From Fox Park in Plymouth, ride east on Warren Street to the stop sign at **0.1 mile**, and turn right onto the pavement of Thurlow Street. The road climbs to the **1.0-mile** mark, where you bear left at a fork onto a dirt road—Old Stagecoach Road. In another 30 yards, turn right onto a double-track trail and enjoy the relatively easy downhill to more pavement at **1.6 miles**. (Stay straight at an

Mount Cardigan and Newfound Lake.

intersection at **1.5 miles**.) Continue straight, passing a hiking trail on the right (no bikes) that leads up Glove Hollow Brook to Rainbow Falls. The pavement starts with a steep uphill on its way to an intersection with Texas Hill Road at **2.2 miles**. Continue straight on the dirt road, riding downhill through forests and past farms where you might spot wild turkeys foraging.

At **3.7 miles**, turn right onto another paved road and follow it to Hunt Road at **4.7 miles**, where you turn right. This dirt road climbs steadily and becomes rocky double-track at **5.1 miles**, where a driveway bends to the right and Hunt Road (which is in worse shape than the driveway) continues straight. At **5.2 miles**, another driveway bends to the left—continue straight, leaving civilization behind. Continuing uphill over moderately technical terrain, the

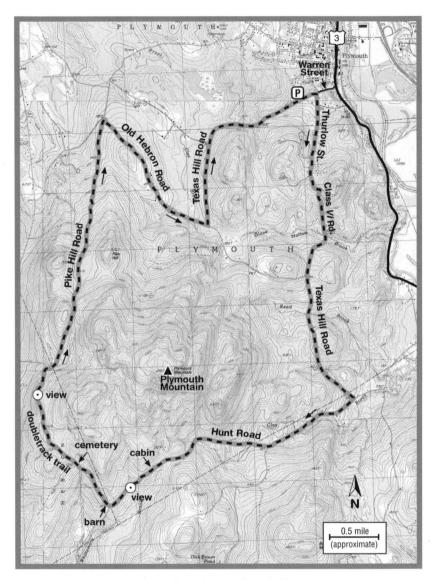

PLYMOUTH MOUNTAIN

road crosses a stream at **5.5 miles** in a scenic forest of hardwoods and hemlocks. Reach the high point of Hunt Road at **5.8 miles,** where you pass a cabin and a clearcut with views to the summit of Plymouth Mountain. It is then a downhill ride to a road, a barn, and a view of Newfound Lake at **6.8 miles.** Turn right and follow the grassy double-track to the right of the barn.

It is a relatively easy uphill ride to the old cemetery at **7.5 miles.** In the nineteenth century, the fields along this old road were farmed; this cemetery is a small reminder that this part of Hebron was once settled. Revolutionary War medallions adorn two of the headstones, connecting this ride to New Hampshire's colonial past. There are no longer farms along this road, just forested hillside. Beyond the cemetery, the trail levels off and then descends, passing two snowmobile trails before reaching a break in the trees at **8.1 miles,** where there is an excellent view of Mount Cardigan rising above the blue waters of Newfound Lake. Continue the descent over a sometimes rocky trail to a dirt road at **8.4 miles,** where you turn right.

At **8.6 miles,** the road bends to the left, but you continue straight on a Class VI road that climbs Pike Hill. Pike Hill Road is relatively easy double-track with some moderate sections as it climbs past trail junctions at **8.7** and **9.3 miles,** where it begins to head downhill; continue straight. After another trail leads to the left at **10.0 miles,** Pike Hill Road continues to descend over a moderately rocky roadbed, with some short, very technical sections. At **11.2 miles,** turn right onto Old Hebron Road—an easy-to-ride dirt road that climbs for about 0.5 mile before providing a much-deserved downhill run past stone walls, fields, and views of the White Mountains. At **12.9 miles,** turn left onto Texas Hill Road and enjoy a mostly downhill ride on pavement back to your car at **15.0 miles.**

Directions

From I-93, take Exit 26 and head south on US 3. In about 1.6 miles, turn right onto Warren Street. In another 0.4 mile, go straight through a stop sign. In another 0.1 mile, park in the lot at Fox Park on the right.

Springfield to Wilmot

> Aerobic Difficulty: **Strenuous**
>
> Technical Difficulty: **Easy to Moderate**
>
> Distance: **20.0 miles round–trip**
>
> Elevation Gain: **2,200 feet**
>
> Estimated Time: **5 hours**
>
> Maps: **USGS Grafton, New London, Enfield Center, and Sunapee Quadrangles**
>
> **A long ride on country roads and an old logging road with good views of Mounts Cardigan and Kearsarge.**

THIS RIDE THROUGH THE COUNTRYSIDE in Springfield and Wilmot primarily uses dirt back roads and a few miles of pavement, although there is a 3-mile ride over rocky double-track through the Gile Memorial State Forest. There are a few more miles of technically challenging double-track trails in the state forest, but this trip sticks to the gentler, though longer, country roads in the surrounding area. Highlights include excellent views of Mount Cardigan, and visits to a historic church and nearby cemeteries. This is also good moose-watching country. A long ride with 2,200 feet of elevation gain, this is a strenuous trip. No facilities are available.

To start, turn right out of the parking area, heading north on NH 4A. Enjoy a rolling ride on pavement until you reach Old Grafton Road at **3.7 miles**, where you turn right. At **4.3 miles**, follow Old Grafton Road to the right where Deep Snow Road continues straight. As you ride past a metal gate, the road turns to double-track trail that climbs moderately over relatively easy terrain. The trail crosses a stream at **4.9 miles**, then passes an interesting old stone dam on the left. Crest the height-of-land at about **5.7 miles**, where an old hunting

The North Wilmot Church was built in 1829.

camp is on the left. Beyond the height-of-land, the trail drops steeply; you will need to negotiate a challenging route around rocks, over water bars, and through deep ruts created by off-road vehicles. Occasionally, there are glimpses of Mount Cardigan to the north. Except for a short, steep uphill section at about **6.0 miles,** it is downhill all the way to **7.4 miles,** where you pass a beaver pond and then make a short climb to the end of a dirt road that dead-ends at the Kinsman Highway at **7.7 miles.**

Here you enjoy the best view of the trip—a beautiful look at Mount Cardigan rising above the farms of Grafton. Turn right for a smooth downhill ride to pavement at **8.8 miles,** where the Kinsman Highway crosses a stream and then turns left. The road continues its descent to Slab City Road at **9.5 miles,** where you turn right. Slab City Road is a rolling dirt road that dead-ends into Dean Hill Road at **10.8 miles.** Turn right onto Dean Hill Road, another dirt road that climbs moderately until **12.7 miles,** then proceeds downhill through forests and past farms, including one that offers a good view of Mount Kearsarge. At **13.7 miles,** turn right onto Old North Road,

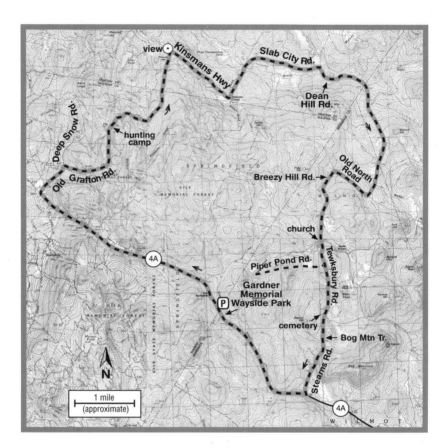

SPRINGFIELD–WILMOT

which rolls along past more of the same scenery on its way to Breezy Hill Road at **14.4 miles.** Turn left and follow this road downhill to the old North Wilmot Church at **15.7 miles.**

The North Wilmot Church is a beautiful white-steepled structure built in 1829 and still serving the local community, which is smaller now than it was in the mid-nineteenth century. From the church, you can take a side trip to Piper Pond by taking a right onto Piper Pond Road. In about 1.0 mile you will reach Piper Pond, a scenic pond surrounded by pines, spruce, hardwoods, and small hills. This road connects to trails in the state forest, but we found it to be impassable due to a beaver pond about 1.3 miles west of the church. If you opt to skip this side trip, ride south from the church on Tewksbury Road, which climbs steeply to the old Tewksbury

Cemetery (also from 1829) and good views of Mount Kearsarge at **16.2 miles.** The road then makes a fun descent over a good dirt surface. If you are not going too fast, you can check out the old Stearns cemetery at **16.9 miles,** just before Tewksbury Road becomes Stearns Road where Sawyer Road leads left.

Continue straight on Stearns Road. At **17.4 miles,** you pass the Kimpton Brook and Bog Mountain Trails (see trip #2); at **18.0 miles,** reach pavement at NH 4A. Turn right and ride the final 2.0 miles of the trip back to the parking area, which will be on your right. Just before you reach your vehicle, you will see an old dam tailrace along Kimpton Brook on the right.

Directions

From I-89, take Exit 11 and head east on NH 11. In 7.1 miles, turn left onto NH 4A. In another 7.1 miles, park on the right in the Gardner Memorial Wayside Park.

6
quietwater paddling

SOUTHERN NEW HAMPSHIRE is rich in paddling opportunities, with lakes, ponds, and rivers in practically every town. Still, finding quiet water for a relaxing paddle on a summer weekend is not always easy—all of the larger lakes and many of the smaller ones allow motorboats and Jet Skis. For this chapter, we searched out the quiet places where you can paddle peacefully among water lilies and purple pickerelweed while watching loons and painted turtles. Or look for otters, mink, muskrats, great blue herons, ospreys, and countless songbirds. All of the trips in this chapter are suitable for both solo paddlers and families.

Paddling Tips

Paddling the ponds in southern New Hampshire is a fairly safe activity. To ensure an accident-free and comfortable paddling experience, however, consider the following tips:

- Know how to use your canoe or kayak. Small lakes and ponds are the perfect place for inexperienced paddlers to learn, but if you are new to the sport, you should at least have someone show you the basic paddling strokes and impress upon you how best to enter and exit your particular boat. New paddlers should consider staying close to shore until they are more comfortable with their paddling skills. Luckily, some of the most interesting aspects of the trips in this chapter are found along the shoreline.

- Turn around before the members of your party start feeling tired. Paddling a few miles after your arms are already spent can make for cranky travel. All of the trips in this book start and end at the same location, so you can easily turn around at any time.

- Make sure everyone in your group is wearing a Coast Guard–approved, properly fitting personal flotation device (PFD). It is very easy to accidentally tip a canoe, especially if the wind kicks up 2-foot waves, and because you can be a long way from shore, it just makes sense to be wearing a PFD.

- Be cautious around motorboats on Pawtuckaway Lake, where large boats can create big wakes. If you fear you might get swamped by such a wake, turn the bow of your boat into the waves. Also, do not assume that bigger boats can see you. Kayaks especially can be hard to spot in bright sunlight or fog, so it might be up to you to get out of the way.

- Pay close attention to the winds. Winds as gentle as 10 miles per hour can create some fairly large waves on some of these ponds. Be prepared for the possibility of a change in the weather—calm days can turn suddenly choppy. Bring a wind-breaker, because it can get cold in a canoe in the lightest of winds. The Pillsbury Ponds, Hubbard Pond, Copps Pond, and Manning Lake are good choices for a windy day.

- Stay off the water if thunderstorms are nearby. Lightning is a serious danger to boaters. If you hear a thunderstorm approaching, get off of the water immediately and seek shelter. For a current weather forecast, call the National Weather Service at 603-225-5191.

- Bring the following supplies with you to make the trip more comfortable. Why not when you don't have to carry them on your back?

Water—one or two quarts per person depending on the weather and length of the trip

Food—Even for a one-hour paddle, it is a good idea to bring some high-energy snacks such as nuts, dried fruit, or snack bars; bring a lunch for longer trips

Map and compass, and the ability to use them

Extra clothing—rain gear, wool sweater, or fleece jacket, wool or fleece hat

Flashlight

Sunscreen and hat

First-aid kit

Pocketknife

Binoculars for wildlife viewing

Field guide such as The Sibley Guide to Birds *by David Sibley*

In addition to the no-impact techniques described in chapter 1, please keep the following things in mind while paddling:

- Give wildlife a wide berth. Lakes and ponds are much different than forests in that wildlife has less of an opportunity to hide from humans. The summer months see a lot of people in the water, and the ducks, herons, and loons waste a good deal of energy just swimming or flying away from curious boaters. If you spot wildlife, remain still and quiet and let the animals decide whether or not to approach you. Use binoculars if you want a closer view. In spring, steer well clear of loons nesting along the shore.

- Respect private property. Much of the land surrounding the ponds in this chapter is private property. Also, most of the put-ins are adjacent to private property, so please act with respect in order to ensure access for future paddlers. Do not land your boat on private property; speak quietly when paddling near houses and cottages.

- Respect the purity of the water. Some of these ponds are used for drinking water by the surrounding communities. If you need to relieve yourself, try to do so on land, at least 200 yards from the shoreline.

- Sound carries a long way on the water, so try to keep your conversations quiet in order to not disturb other paddlers or nearby hikers.

Paddling Times and Distances

The distances listed on our trips basically assume you will follow the shoreline of the pond for most of the trip. Trips will be shorter in distance if you paddle directly from Point A to Point B and back, but we expect that most people like to explore the shoreline for at least part of a trip to look for animals, flowers, and resting spots. Paddling times can vary widely based on paddlers' experience, physical conditioning, and curiosity. We have tried to come up with the time it would take a paddler of average strength and experience to complete these trips with only one short rest break to eat a snack. If you have a group of very curious paddlers, expect your trips to take longer.

A quietwater paddle in southern New Hampshire often consists of floating among reeds and cattails while staring off into the distance toward Mount Cardigan or the Belknap Range. The up-close details are more even more enticing—bass swimming beneath your paddles as green frogs float on fragrant water lilies. In spring and early summer you are likely to find swallows swooping in front of your path and colorful warblers, orioles, and tanagers singing from branches hanging over the shoreline. And just when the surrounding woods start to get quiet in fall, the hardwoods start to change from green to red, yellow, and orange, creating a new incentive to get out every day and dip those paddles in the water.

Copps Pond

> Distance: **1.5 miles round–trip**
>
> Estimated Time: **1 hour**
>
> Map: **USGS Melvin Village Quadrangle**
>
> **Turtles, frogs, ducks, and lily pads are common sights on this short, easy paddle.**

SMALL, SHALLOW COPPS POND is the perfect choice if you are looking for a short paddle in the Lakes Region away from big waves, big boats, and big summer homes. The pond is part of a state wildlife management area that is used by duck hunters in fall. Between 100 and 150 acres of this area can be paddled, depending on the time of year, because the cattails, water lilies, and other plants make parts of the pond impassable later in summer. Kayakers will definitely want to keep their rudders in the "up" position on this pond, as they will just collect plant life and slow you down. All of these water plants make great hiding places for wildlife such as green frogs, bullfrogs, brook trout, and ducks.

There are two buildings on the northern shore but the shoreline is otherwise undeveloped. Southern and western reaches feel the wildest, with hardwoods rising from the shoreline on the surrounding low-lying hills. The trout and frogs, as well as hordes of dragonflies and damselflies, lure avian predators such as great blue herons, kingfishers, kingbirds, and tree swallows. Mink patrol the shoreline and the small islands in the pond, while snapping turtles hunt from below. Judging by the scrapings we saw on the sandy banks near the put-in, the snappers nest here as well. No facilities are available.

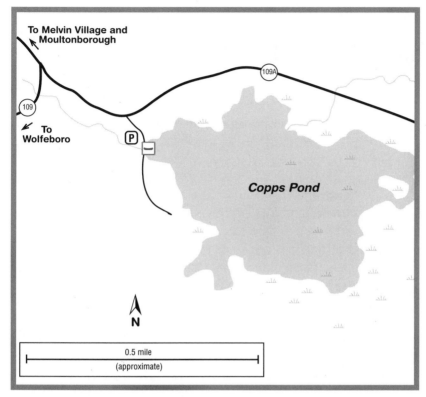

COPPS POND

Directions

From the intersection of NH 109 and NH 109A in Tuftonboro, head south on NH 109A. In about 0.3 mile, turn right onto a dirt road and park in about 200 yards next to the NH Fish and Game sign.

Also Nearby

If you finish this trip and feel the need to keep your boat wet, you can paddle Moultonborough Bay on Lake Winnipesaukee by using the boat ramp in nearby Melvin Village on NH 109. Expect to share the lake with powerboats, and be prepared for big waves in windy conditions.

Snappers: Predators from the Murky Depths

SNAPPING TURTLES SEEM TO BE about the scariest turtles around with their sharp, beaklike mouths that snap repeatedly when they are disturbed on land. Even the *Peterson Field Guide to Reptiles and Amphibians* describes snappers as "ugly both in appearance and disposition." In the water, however, snapping turtles are much more docile. Luckily for swimmers, they either swim away or just pull in their heads when underwater, letting people step on them and pass by unknowingly. Paddlers lucky enough to see one swimming will also realize that they can be quite graceful swimmers.

Snapping turtles reach lengths of 18 inches, weigh up to 75 pounds, and can live as long as 100 years. They are easily recognized by their large heads, beaklike mouths, long tails, and very rough brownish black shells. They are voracious omnivores, eating small invertebrates, fish, reptiles, small birds, mammals, and vegetation. They will live in any permanent body of fresh water. They are most likely to be seen on land in June or July, when the females lay a clutch of ten to twenty-five eggs. The eggs hatch in September or October.

Eggs maintained in the low-seventy-degree range become males; those maintained at warmer or cooler temperatures become females.

A snapping turtle looking for a nesting site.

Willard Pond

> **Distance: 2.0 miles round-trip**
>
> **Estimated Time: 2 hours**
>
> Map: **USGS Stoddard Quadrangle**
>
> **Glacial erratics line the shoreline of this pond surrounded by hills and home to loons and ospreys.**

WILLARD POND DEFINES *QUIET WATER.* Motorboats are prohibited in the pond, which is about 100 acres in size and nestled between Bald Mountain and Goodhue Hill in Antrim. Glacial erratics covered in lichens line the shoreline, and the surrounding forest is alive with bird activity. There is one small cabin near the put-in, but otherwise the land bordering the pond is building-free. The seclusion of Willard Pond is protected by New Hampshire Audubon's dePierrefeu-Willard Pond Wildlife Sanctuary, which at 1,000-plus acres is the Audubon Society of New Hampshire's largest sanctuary. In addition to the sanctuary there are another 1,000 acres of protected land near the pond, so the plant life and wildlife you encounter on a paddle here are ensured of a place to live. For more information, you can contact New Hampshire Audubon at 603-224-9909, www.nhaudubon.org.

It is easy to explore the entire shoreline of Willard Pond in an hour or two, making it an ideal early-morning paddle that can be completed before getting on with the rest of the day. Loons nest on the pond—be on the lookout in spring for their nesting sites and make an effort to keep your distance. In addition to loons, we saw great blue herons, kingfishers, and ospreys while paddling here, so the fish supply must be plentiful. The pond is also home to red-spotted newts—in spring look for their egg masses near the northern shore of the pond, where there is a marshy inlet to the pond as well

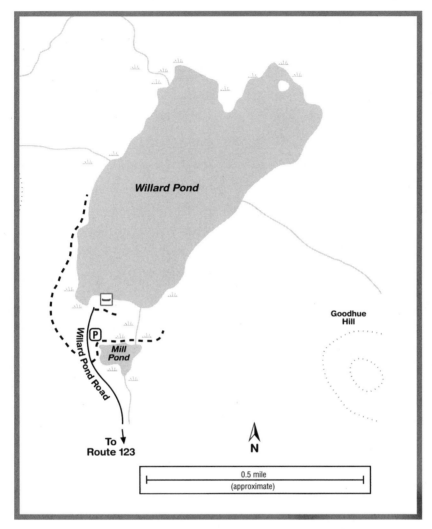

WILLARD POND

as an old stone wall. Swimming is not allowed in the pond, and the eastern shoreline is private property. If you need to land your boat, use the western shore, which is part of the Audubon sanctuary. No facilities are available.

Directions

From the south: From the northern intersection of NH 137 and NH 123 in Hancock, head north on NH 123. In 3.1 miles, turn right onto Davenport Road. In another 0.7 mile, take the left fork, which will be Willard Pond Road. The road dead-ends into the pond in about 1.0 mile, but park in the lot on the left about 200 yards before the pond.

From the north: From the intersection of NH 9 and NH 123, head south on NH 123. In 3.4 miles, turn left onto Willard Pond Road and drive 1.7 miles to the pond.

Also Nearby

This paddle can be combined with a hike up Bald Mountain ($2^1/2$ hours) or Goodhue Hill ($1^1/2$ hours). The trails for both start near the parking area for Willard Pond. The views of the Monadnock Region from Bald Mountain are exceptional. Trail maps are available at the trailhead.

Manning Lake

> Distance: **2.5 miles round–trip**
>
> Estimated Time: **1 1/2 hours**
>
> Map: **USGS Gilmanton Ironworks Quadrangle**
>
> **A short paddle among lily pads and over crystal–clear water with good views of the Belknap Range.**

MANNING LAKE IS RELATIVELY SMALL at 200 acres, making it more an afternoon or early-morning adventure than an all-day paddle, but it is the perfect antidote to the frenzy of summer on nearby Lake Winnipesaukee. A few houses dot the shoreline and a youth camp has some frontage on the eastern shore, but this is a relatively quiet place with a simple beauty worth visiting. The lake is very clean, and you can often see down to the sandy bottom where freshwater mussels grow in clumps—the mink and otter must have a large diet of shellfish in this lake.

The rocky shoreline of the lake is buffered by pickerelweed, yellow pond lilies, and fragrant water lilies. On a sunny summer day, the colors of these flowers blend magically with the blue reflection of the sky and with the blue and green dragonflies drifting from lily pad to lily pad. In the shallows, it is common to see small fish darting among the vegetation, while in the deep water in the coves at the south end of the lake you might see large bass and pickerel swimming in and out of the shadows. Once you look up from the depths, you will notice the peaks of the Belknap Range only a few miles away. No facilities are available.

Manning Lake.

Directions

From NH 11 and NH 140 in Alton, head west on NH 140. In about 5.4 miles, just past the center of Gilmanton Ironworks, turn right onto Crystal Lake Road. In 3.2 miles, continue straight as the road becomes Guinea Pond Road. In another 1.8 miles, turn right onto a dirt road, Manning Lake Road. The put-in is on the right in about 0.6 mile.

Also Nearby

While Manning Lake is quiet, its small size may leave you hungry for more paddling. Nearby Sunset and Crystal Lakes are much more developed, but can still provide hours afloat. Sunset Lake is just east of Manning Lake on Alton Mountain Road, while the put-in for Crystal Lake is on Crystal Lake Road just north of NH 140.

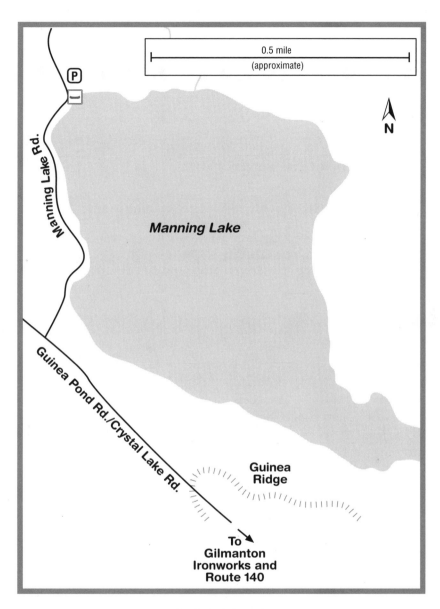

0.5 mile
(approximate)

N

P

Manning Lake Rd.

Manning Lake

Guinea Pond Rd./Crystal Lake Rd.

Guinea
Ridge

To
Gilmanton
Ironworks and
Route 140

MANNING LAKE

Pillsbury State Park Ponds

> **Distance: 2.5 miles round–trip with longer options;
> includes 150–yard portage**
> Estimated Time: **2 hours**
> Map: **USGS Lovewell Mountain Quadrangle**
>
> **A paddle across one pond with a portage to
> a second, completely secluded pond
> surrounded by bogs, hills, and hardwoods.**

PILLSBURY STATE PARK in Washington is one of New Hampshire's lesser-known parks, but it should be high on any visitor's list of places to visit in the southern part of the state. Park activities focus on the four ponds that are accessible to paddlers. Pondside campsites are available, including a few remote sites on North Pond. In addition to paddling, the park also offers some good mountain biking and hiking trails, including access to the Monadnock-Sunapee Greenway. (Trip #1 describes the short hike to Balance Rock.) You can paddle Butterfield and May Ponds from the put-in next to the park office, but we will describe the paddle on Mill and North Ponds. A picnic area and pit toilets are located near the put-in.

From the parking area next to Mill Pond, you can easily explore the shoreline of the entire pond in about thirty minutes. It is a shallow pond filled with water lilies and reeds, red-spotted newts and beaver lodges. The real lure of this trip, however, is remote North Pond and its completely undeveloped shoreline. Paddle to the northern end of Mill Pond, where you will find a portage trail just to the left of the inlet to the pond. Carry your boat the 150 yards through the woods to North Pond and put in to the right of the campsite at the end of the portage trail.

North Pond has a feeling of complete seclusion. It sits in a bowl surrounded by the hills and drumlins of the Sunapee Range.

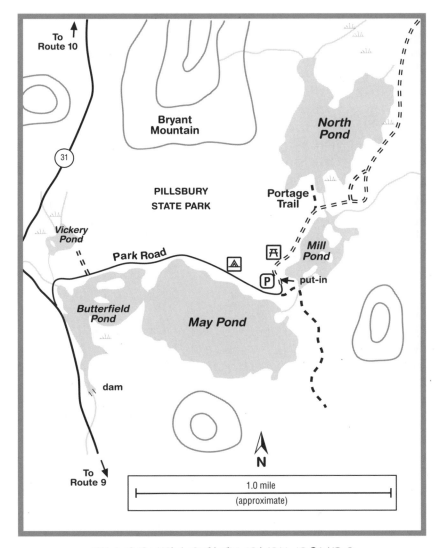

PILLSBURY STATE PARK PONDS

The shoreline consists of tall spruce and white pines with a few colorful red maples thrown in. In the middle of the pond are some boggy islands with narrow channels between them that make for some interesting exploring. The bogs are covered in heathlike plants such as sheep laurel as well as blueberries, cotton grass, larch, sphagnum moss, and the carnivorous pitcher plant. Beaver lodges rise up out of the sides of the bogs, providing the beavers with a safe, predator-free environment. The shoreline surrounding the pond is rather rocky, but there are plenty of places where it is possible to land a boat and take a break.

Directions

From Washington, head north on NH 31. In 4.1 miles, turn right into Pillsbury State Park. The put-in is at the parking area in the cul-de-sac at the end of the park road in 1.4 miles. There is a fee to enter the park.

Ospreys and Bald Eagles: Back in New Hampshire

OSPREY AND BALD EAGLE numbers are both increasing in New Hampshire, but both birds are still relatively rare in the state. Bald eagles are easily identified as they are our largest bird of prey and have a wingspan of nearly 7 feet. Eagles have a brown body with a conspicuous white head and tail. Osprey have only partially white heads with a thick, dark eyestripe. They have dark brown backs and white undersides, and they are much smaller than eagles, with a wingspan of about 5 feet. While these large birds of prey are distinctly dissimilar in appearance, they share many common habits and habitats. These similarities often put them in close proximity to one another, resulting in regular battles for prey and territory. While the bald eagle is our nation's symbol, the osprey tends to be held in higher regard by naturalists and biologists because it is a pure and successful hunter. Ospreys catch fish more than 50 percent of the time they try, and they rarely eat anything else. Bald eagles, on the other hand, are less successful hunters and will feast on carrion any chance they get. They also follow and harass ospreys in an attempt to steal their catch. In fact, Ben Franklin once observed: "I wish the Bald Eagle had not been chosen as the representative of our country. He is a bird of bad moral character; he does not get his living honestly. Besides he is a rank coward."

Of course, the bald eagle is one of our country's most magnificent animals, soaring gracefully on thermals with an 8-foot wingspan and possessing beautiful and regal coloring. Adults mate for life and share in the parenting duties, raising broods of two chicks in huge nests that are used year after year. They nest in the tallest trees they can find, usually a white pine or spruce, near any large body of water that is sufficiently free of human disturbance. Older nests can weigh as much as a ton and will usually end up killing the tree in which they are situated. The birds do not grow their distinctive white tail and head feathers until they are four or five years old. Until that time they are either mottled in appearance or sport a completely brown coloring, resembling golden eagles. Bald eagles had not nested in New Hampshire for several decades before a pair built a nest on the New Hampshire side of Lake Umbagog in the 1990s. In 2000 there were nests on Umbagog, the Pontook Reservoir, Spoonbill Pond, and the Connecticut River, but none of them successfully fledged chicks. Two more pairs showed signs of nest-building activity on the Merrimack River and Squam Lake. Despite the lack of young, biologists are excited about the increase in nesting activity, as these birds will most likely attempt to nest again in the years to come. About twenty bald eagles spend the winter roosting in the trees around the open waters of Great Bay.

Like bald eagles, the smaller ospreys prefer to nest in tall trees near water in relatively wild areas. They are somewhat more adaptable than eagles, sometimes nesting closer to civilization on telephone poles or other tall artificially constructed structures that give them an open view of their surroundings. They are also more likely to nest next to small ponds that are fish rich. They mate for life and like the eagle, both parents raise the young.

Ospreys are currently the lucky beneficiaries of the first-ever recovery plan written for an endangered species in New Hampshire. Called Project Osprey, the plan is being managed cooperatively by the New Hampshire Fish and Game Department, the Audubon Society of New Hampshire, and Public Service of New Hampshire (whose utility poles are sometimes chosen as nesting sites by ospreys). The project's goal is to foster a self-sustaining osprey population in the state within five years. In 2000 there were about twenty-five nesting pairs that fledged forty chicks. Ospreys may be seen on many of the paddles in this book; Great Bay is the best bet, because at least two pairs nest in the area. It is common to find eagles and ospreys nesting in sight of each other, which results in constant aerial battles. While the birds seldom hurt each other, ospreys will harass and dive at eagles flying in their vicinity. Groups of ravens, peregrine falcons, and other birds of prey will also harass eagles in order to get them to leave an area. These displays are quite exciting to watch and usually end with the eagle deciding to catch a thermal and fly to more peaceful surroundings.

Bald eagle populations declined consistently from the time Europeans arrived in North America until the 1940s as a result of persecution by hunters, anglers, and farmers. Ospreys, on the other hand, managed to escape some of this persecution because farmers believed their presence kept away smaller falcons such as merlins and kestrels, which prey on domestic fowl. After World War II, both birds met considerable peril due to the widespread use of DDT and other pollutants. These chemicals do not kill the birds, but are stored in their fatty tissues and eventually reach a level that creates reproductive problems. Eggs laid by birds with high concentrations of DDT had thin shells and often ended up being crushed during incubation. Since the ban on DDT, the birds' reproductive success has improved in most of the country. At this time, the greatest threat to both ospreys and eagles is habitat loss.

Trip #32

Hubbard Pond

> Distance: **3.5 miles round–trip**
>
> Estimated Time: **2 hours**
>
> Map: **USGS Peterborough South Quadrangle**
>
> **An interesting paddle among bogs, beavers, birds, and good views of Mount Monadnock.**

HUBBARD POND is the least developed of the numerous ponds and lakes in the area around the southern New Hampshire towns of Rindge and Jaffrey. While there is a Boy Scout camp on its western shore, the rest of the pond lies within the borders of the Annett State Forest and is therefore free of development. The pond is long and narrow with numerous marshy coves providing plenty of seclusion and possibilities for nature study. The pond is also very shallow; travel can get sticky in late summer when the vegetation has had a chance to grow thick. Paddle in spring or fall or bring a boat without much draft. Paddling in the off-season also ensures that you will not be sharing the pond with the sounds of Boy Scouts.

Hubbard Pond is both quiet and pretty. Tall white and red pines surround the water, which is choked with blooming water lilies. As you paddle south, good views open up to Mount Monadnock rising above the trees in the northwest. There are also several islands that barely rise above the surface of the water, providing boggy habitat suitable for sheep laurel, blueberries, and cotton grass, as well as scrubby black spruce and larch trees. Heron, beaver, and muskrat are common here; in spring and early summer the bird life is fairly prolific. Because most of the land around the pond is part of the state forest, it is acceptable to land your boat for a picnic or rest break—the eastern shore is your best bet. No facilities area available.

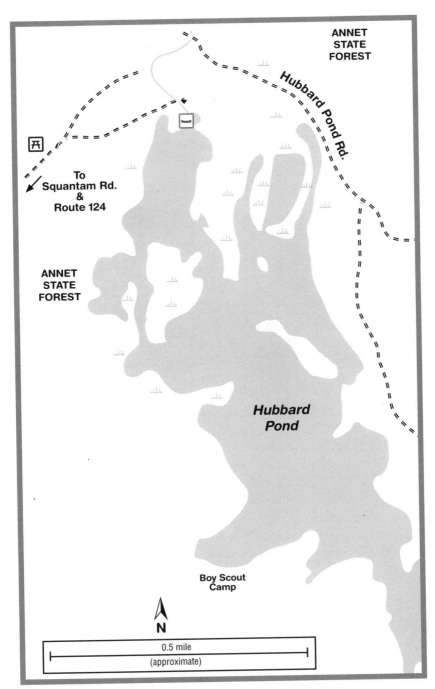

ANNET
STATE
FOREST

Hubbard Pond Rd.

To
Squantam Rd.
&
Route 124

ANNET
STATE
FOREST

*Hubbard
Pond*

Boy Scout
Camp

N

0.5 mile
(approximate)

HUBBARD POND

Water lilies float in a quiet cove on Hubbard Pond.

Directions

From the intersection of NH 124 and US 202 in Jaffrey, head east on NH 124. In 2.2 miles, turn right onto Prescott Road. In another 0.7 mile, turn left onto Squantam Road. In 0.6 mile, just past the sign for Annett State Forest, turn left onto an unnamed dirt road. The put-in is at the end of this road in about 0.5 mile. Please note that this is a rough four-wheel-drive road that can be difficult to pass, especially in spring or after heavy rains.

Grafton Pond

> **Distance: 5 miles round-trip**
> **Estimated Time: 3 hours**
> **Map: USGS Enfield Center Quadrangle**
>
> **A half-day paddle among pine-covered islands and wildlife-filled coves.**

GRAFTON POND IS ONE OF THOSE GEMS where you can spend as much time as you like exploring nooks and crannies or sunning yourself on a rock on the shore of an island in the middle of the pond. The few houses near the dam at the put-in seem to quickly disappear as you paddle out among the islands on this 235-acre pond that seems much larger. Except for the northwestern shore, most of the land around Grafton Pond is protected by the Society for the Protection of New Hampshire Forests' 940-acre Grafton Pond Reservation. Thanks to the society's foresight in 1984, Grafton Pond is still a wild place with crystal-clear waters and abundant wildlife.

From the put-in, you can paddle in either direction and end up having a worthwhile paddle. Deep coves at both the northern and southern ends of the pond are great places to watch for wildlife such as beaver, mink, heron, and turtle. The white pines on the immediate shoreline give way to a northern hardwood forest on the surrounding hillsides. There are numerous places to pull up and enjoy a sunny picnic, although camping is not allowed on the islands or in the preserve. Unsettling-sized waves can pick up on a windy day here, although you will be relatively safe because no spot on the lake is more than a few hundred yards from shore.

The biggest risk of being out in the middle of the pond is looking out toward the bald summit of Mount Cardigan and deciding you need to call in sick and go for a hike the next day! There are pit toilets in the parking area.

Kayakers explore one of the numerous coves in the wild and scenic waters of Grafton Pond.

Directions

From Proctor's General Store in Enfield Center, head east on NH 4A. In 2.3 miles, turn left onto Grafton Pond Road. In about 0.9 mile, the road forks—take the right fork, following a sign that says "Scenic Rd." In another 1.0 mile, turn right at a T-intersection onto a dirt road. The parking area is just beyond the dam in a few hundred yards.

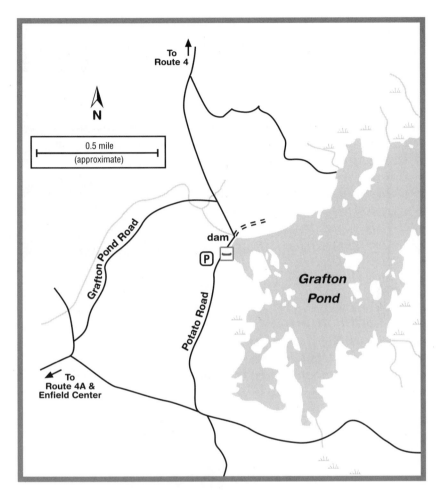

GRAFTON POND

The Great Blue Heron

STANDING 4 FEET TALL with a wingspan of 6 feet, the great blue heron is the largest heron in the United States, and it is the third largest bird in our region after bald and golden eagles. (Sandhill cranes are also larger, but they are only occasional migrants.) They are easy birds to identify: they are the only 4-foot-tall bird around with a blue-gray body, black-and-white head, cinnamon-brown and white neck, and long buffy-gray legs. In flight, they tuck their neck in close to their body, beat their huge wings very slowly, and trail their legs behind their body, often making loud croaking calls. They are commonly seen on all of the paddling trips in this book, as they feed in rivers, ponds, and marshes, standing still or slowly stalking fish, frogs, salamanders, snakes, small birds, rodents, and insects.

Great blue herons were heading toward extinction 100 years ago when, like most herons and egrets, they were hunted for their feathers, then used as fashion accessories. In 1900 Congress passed the Lacey Act, which prohibited the interstate commercial trade of feathers. This law and the Migratory Bird Treaty Act of 1918 contributed greatly to the great blue heron's comeback. Today a few thousand of these birds nest in northern New England, most of them in large rookeries that range in size from a few nesting pairs to several hundred. Often sharing their rookeries with other herons and egret species, great blue herons build large stick nests in the tops of trees. They usually line the nest with reeds, mosses, and grasses to help protect the three to five eggs, one or two of which grow to fledge between nine and thirteen weeks.

Great blue heron with catfish.

Stay clear of rookeries during nesting season, which is usually from late April through early August. Disturbing herons during this time can decrease their chances of successfully raising young. If that's not enough motivation, remember that when they are upset, herons will sometimes regurgitate the contents of their stomach onto the offending party. Despite their 100-year rise to "common" status, great blue herons are still at risk due to habitat loss and toxic waste, which makes its way through the food chain, accumulating in the tissues of adult birds, eventually making it impossible for them to produce healthy chicks. Happily, for now great blue herons are a common sight that we can observe with wonder during the entire paddling season.

Pawtuckaway Lake

> **Distance: 5 miles round-trip, with longer options**
> **Estimated Time: 3 hours**
> **Map: USGS Mount Pawtuckaway Quadrangle**
>
> **Pines, loons, and mountain views on the secluded northern end of this large lake.**

PAWTUCKAWAY STATE PARK is full of recreation opportunities—camping, fishing, hiking, mountain biking, and paddling. (See trips #8 and #20 for hiking and biking suggestions.) Most of the activity on Pawtuckaway Lake is concentrated at its southern end, which includes the park's campground and beach area, both of which get a lot of use in summer. This southern end also sees a fair amount of motorboat and Jet Ski activity. This trip focuses on the quiet northern end of the lake. Here you are more likely to encounter great blue herons and loons than Jet Skis. There are pit toilets at the put-in.

The put-in at the north end of the lake is in Fundy Cove, a narrow slice of water surrounded by tall white pine and highbush blueberry. At the south end of the cove are two boggy islands that barely rise above the surface of the water, but have enough soil on them to support large numbers of blueberry bushes and small birds such as song sparrows, tree swallows, and red-winged blackbirds. By turning left at these two islands, you head toward the main part of the lake, which is at the end of a channel, beyond Log Cabin Island. Here is where you need to make a choice: To the right of Log Cabin Island lies the bulk of the lake, including the state park beach area. To the left are a couple more coves that stay quiet most days of the year and are home to nesting loons and insect eaters like kingbirds, cedar waxwings, and Baltimore orioles. You also get a nice view of Mount Pawtuckaway. At the far end of the easternmost cove are a

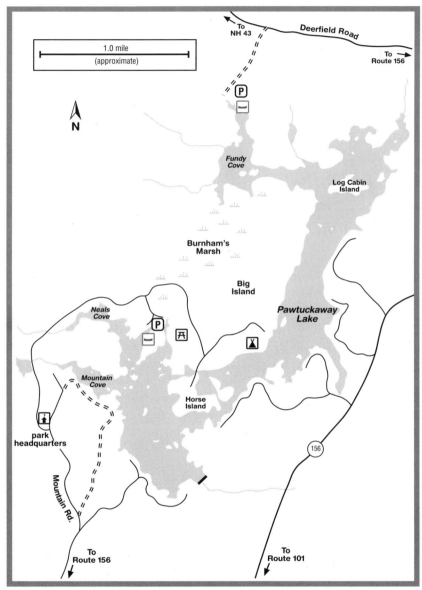

PAWTUCKAWAY LAKE

dam and a small town beach. (Please do not land your boat on the beach—it is for Nottingham residents only.)

If it seems to be a quiet day, you can head south and explore the rest of the lake, which is about 3 miles long. Winds out of the north can create some pretty big waves as you get near the southern end, so watch the weather and plan accordingly.

Directions

From NH 156 and NH 152 in Nottingham, head south on NH 156. In 1.0 mile, turn right onto Deerfield Road. In another 2.0 miles, turn left onto an unnamed road marked by a boat-launch sign. The launch is at the end of the road in about 0.5 mile. It is a large lot, but it can get busy on weekends, so start your day early. There is also a put-in on the southern end of the lake in the main section of Pawtuckaway State Park (see map).

Merrymeeting Marsh

> **Distance: 8.0 miles out and back**
>
> **Estimated Time: 4 hours**
>
> **Map: USGS Alton Quadrangle**
>
> **A twisting paddle through a marsh rich in wildlife.**

MERRYMEETING MARSH is the slow-moving cattail-lined part of the Merrymeeting River that flows next to NH 11 in Alton. The river drains Merrymeeting Lake to the north and flows into Lake Winnipesaukee at Alton Bay. This portion of the river borders the Merrymeeting State Wildlife Management Area, which protects valuable habitat for the migrating ducks that attract scores of duck hunters in fall. This trip begins from the state boat launch on NH 11, but it is also possible to paddle the river closer to Merrymeeting Lake by putting in at the boat launch on Merrymeeting Lake Road. No facilities are available.

Despite the fact that you are never more than 0.5 mile from the road, this paddle has a good backwoods feel for the first 2 miles as it makes turn after turn through the marsh, which is bordered by tall white pines and oaks. After the 2-mile mark, you start seeing more civilization as you get nearer the town of Alton. You can paddle as far as the NH 140 bridge—about 4.5 miles from the put-in—passing under NH 28 at 3.5 miles. Instead of heading toward town, you can also explore the deeper recesses of the marsh by turning left and heading up Coffin Brook about 0.5 mile from the put-in, where the river makes a right-hand turn.

As you follow the Merrymeeting to the right, you will find good views of nearby hills as well as a glimpse of Mount Major as you get closer to NH 28, but we had the most fun watching the wildlife around each bend in the marsh—otters, muskrats, beavers,

Merrymeeting Marsh.

herons, mallard ducks, mergansers, and teals. Bring the binoculars for this trip! After your paddle, you can make a visit to the state's Powder Mill Fish Hatchery on Merrymeeting Lake Road, just north of the boat access in New Durham; call 603-673-1416.

Directions

From the rotary at the intersection of NH 28 and NH 11 just south of Alton, head south on NH 11 for 2.4 miles. The put-in will be on your right. To get to the put-in on Merrymeeting Lake Road, continue south on NH 11 for another 0.4 mile and turn left onto Depot Road. In another 0.4 mile, turn left at the stop sign onto Old Bay Road, which becomes Main Street. In another 0.5 mile, turn right onto Merrymeeting Lake Road. The put-in is on the left in 2.3 miles (other put-ins available).

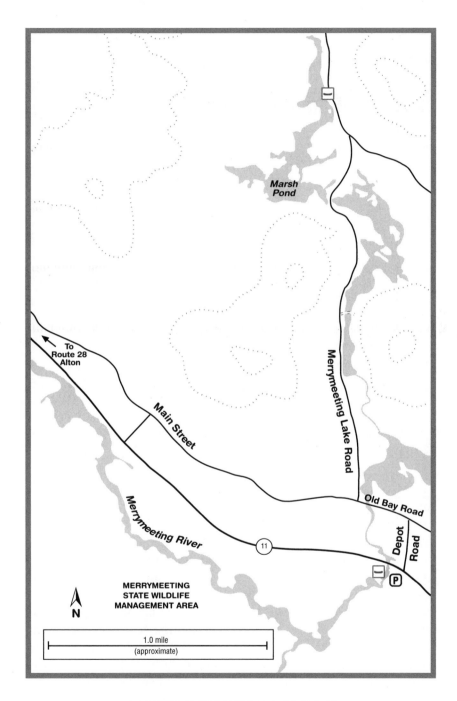

MERRYMEETING MARSH

7

sea kayaking

NEW HAMPSHIRE ONLY HAS ABOUT 17 miles of coastline, but it is has plenty of nooks and crannies that make for interesting one-hour to half-day paddles. The trips in this chapter explore rocky coastline with cobble beaches, the maze of islands near Portsmouth, and a tidal salt marsh creek at Odiorne Point State Park. We have also included Great Bay and Squam Lake in this chapter, because they are big bodies of water that often have oceanlike conditions. You are bound to find wildlife on these paddles, whether it is harbor seals and sea ducks on the open water or shorebirds and mammals such as deer and fox around the islands and salt marsh. What is most remarkable to us as we paddle the coast so close to our home is how quickly we can get a feeling of solitude so close to the busy streets of Portsmouth.

Sea kayaking in the waters of New Hampshire can be safely enjoyed, but not without sufficient training and experience. At its warmest, the water temperature reaches the low sixties—and even at that temperature a submerged paddler can become hypothermic quickly. The weather can also cause problems—especially fog, which can roll in off the ocean at any time—making good navigation skills critical. We feel that to safely sea kayak in New Hampshire, you should have the following minimum level of experience:

- Previous paddling experience in a sea kayak

- Knowledge of the basic paddle strokes: forward, reverse, sweep, skull, brace

- Knowledge of how to use a nautical chart and compass

- Experience at self-rescues and knowledge of how to use a paddle float

Even more experience is needed, however, if you plan on going anywhere near the main channel of the Piscataqua River. The current in this river as it squeezes past Portsmouth and Kittery, Maine, is the second strongest tidal current in the United States. This is big, strong water, with big ship traffic as well. Do not attempt to paddle across the river unless you have a great deal of experience paddling in strong current and have timed your crossing to coincide with favorable tide conditions.

Before putting your boat in the water, you should always check the tide and weather forecasts. Tides are usually listed in local papers such as the *Portsmouth Herald* and *Foster's Daily Democrat*. You can also buy official tide charts at local bookstores. Tides and weather forecasts can be heard on a National Oceanic and Atmospheric Administration (NOAA) weather radio. The NOAA offers excellent long-range forecasts, but for the best up-to-date New Hampshire weather, check the Weather Underground website for Portsmouth: wunderground.com/cgi-bin/findweather/getForecast? query=03801. (This page also links to a marine forecast.) Use common sense and take a look at the conditions when you put your boat in the water. If you see whitecaps on the water, it is probably too windy for a safe and pleasant paddle. Also, if it is foggy at your put-in, choose another trip. Besides causing navigational problems, fog can make you invisible to the many fishing and pleasure boats that travel through the area. Even in sunny conditions, it is advisable to keep your group in a tightly knit formation—this makes you much more visible to boats. *You should never paddle alone.*

Everyone in your group should have the following essential gear with them:

- *Personal flotation device* (PFD)—wear a PFD while sea kayaking in New Hampshire. If you end up in the water, a PFD can save you precious energy that you will need to stave off hypothermia. The few minutes of time a PFD saves you while you try to get back into your boat can save your life.

- *Spare paddle*

- *Paddle float*

- *Sprayskirt*

- *Lunch, snacks, and emergency food*

- *Drinking water*—at least a gallon if you are out for the entire day

- *Sunglasses, sunscreen, and a hat*

- *Appropriate clothing*—dress for the water temperature, not the air temperature. A wet or dry suit is great, but at the least wear synthetic materials and dress in layers. Neoprene or Gore-Tex gloves and booties are also good to have. Do not wear cotton.

- *A dry bag to keep all of the above dry*

You should also carry at least one of each of the following for the entire group:

Compass and charts

First-aid kit

Bilge pump

Foghorn

Flare gun

VHF radio or cell phone (cell phones may not work in all locations)

In addition to paying close attention to safety, kayakers need to follow certain guidelines to avoid having a negative impact on the environment and local residents. First, it is important to respect private property. Never land your boat near a house or on land marked "No Trespassing." You should land your boat only on public property.

Second, give wildlife a wide berth. Seals in particular are easily stressed by kayaks, possibly because kayaks are shaped much like their main predator, killer whales. It is also possible that they have an inherited memory of the days when seals were hunted by people in kayaks. In any event, never approach seals in a kayak, particularly if they are hauled out onto rocks, where they feel especially vulnerable. Try to stay at least 0.5 mile from basking seals. If any animal changes its behavior as you approach, you are too close.

Third, practice Leave No Trace techniques both on and off the water. Pack out all of your trash, including solid human waste. Urinating below the high-tide line is the most effective way to ensure quick dispersal of urine. Do not urinate in a tidal pool, however; this can have negative consequences on the delicate life there. Also, try to stay below the high-tide line at all times to minimize your impact on fragile island habitats. Please do not take rocks and shells home as souvenirs.

Finally, remember that people are out there trying to make a living from fishing. Always let them have the right-of-way and try to stay out of their path. Do not go near lobster traps, and be as quick as possible while using local boat ramps. Theoretically, kayaks have the right-of-way when passing other boats. In practice, larger boats do not always see kayaks or are traveling too fast to change course quickly. Play it safe and move aside when possible.

Only one of these trips is out in the open ocean—trip #39, Rye to Portsmouth. The other trips can all be paddled safely in a kayak or canoe in good weather conditions with favorable tides. By paddling all of these trips, you will see 300-million-year-old rocks bent by crashing continents and squeezed apart by rising magma. You will wander around 180-degree turns hiding herons and egrets and cruise past osprey nests and tall white pines where bald eagles spend the nonbreeding season. You will also paddle "On Golden Pond" (trip #40) with dramatic views of the nearby White Mountains. Enjoy!

Trip #36

Odiorne Salt Marsh

> Difficulty: **Easy**
>
> Distance: **2.5 miles out and back**
>
> Time: **1 hour**
>
> Maps: **USGS Kittery (Maine) Quadrangle, Maptech's Waterproof Chart #27**
>
> **An easy paddle in a tidal creek surrounded by a bird–filled salt marsh.**

WEATHER AND TIDE CONSIDERATIONS: This is a very easy paddle in a tidal creek that is relatively protected from the elements. Because it is tidal, however, plan your trip to avoid low tide, when the creek is reduced to a very shallow, narrow channel surrounded by deep mud flats.

This easy paddle is great when you are up for a short paddle while visiting the area's other attractions. The salt marsh surrounding Seavey Creek and Berrys Brook provides excellent opportunities to watch for shorebirds and wading birds, especially during the spring and fall migrations. This trip is great for bringing the whole family in a canoe. Nearby are Odiorne Point State Park with several miles of hiking trails and New Hampshire Audubon's Seacoast Science Center—a great place to take kids. Restrooms are located in the Science Center, but fees are charged.

From the put-in, paddle left under the wooden bridge and up Seavey Creek. The creek winds its way through the salt marsh for a mile or so, but the nature of the marsh makes it hard to find a direct route, so you may end up paddling more than that as you explore the various channels, pausing often to look through binoculars at great blue herons, snowy egrets, or migrating plovers. You can also explore Berrys Creek by taking a right soon after passing under

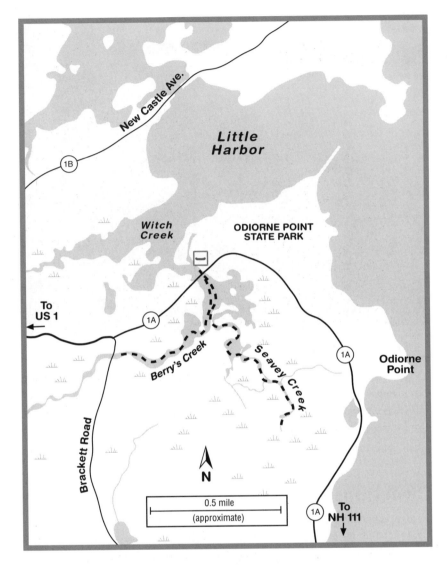

ODIORNE MARSH

the bridge at the put-in. This creek has more marsh to explore and is also bordered by a forest of oak and pine with a few houses on the shoreline. You can paddle up Berrys Creek for about 0.5 mile to a bridge at Brackett Road.

If you feel like more paddling, head into Little Harbor and the nearby islands between New Castle and Portsmouth by paddling

Seavey Creek at high tide.

to the right from the put-in (see trips #37 and #39). Little Harbor does experience strong tidal currents and has deeper water, however, so try this only if you have the requisite experience outlined at the beginning of this chapter.

Directions

From the south: From NH 111 and US 1A in Hampton, head north on US 1A. In 8.1 miles, turn right into the northern entrance to Odiorne Point State Park. A parking fee is charged during the summer. From the north: From US 1A and US 1B in Portsmouth, head south on US 1A. The above parking area will be on the left in 1.6 miles.

Portsmouth Harbor

Difficulty: Easy

Distance: 4.5 miles round-trip

Time: 1 1/2 hours

Maps: USGS Kittery (Maine) Quadrangle, Maptech's Waterproof Chart #27

A quiet exploration of the islands and wooded shoreline between Portsmouth, New Castle, and Rye.

WEATHER AND TIDE CONSIDERATIONS: Paddling during the hours around high tide makes this an easier trip. At low tide, you will be confined to a narrow channel that meanders through mud flats. Between tides, you may encounter some strong currents, particularly around the US 1B bridges at both ends of the loop. This trip is well sheltered for its entire length, although winds of only 10 to 15 knots can begin to make paddling here an unpleasant experience. It can be especially difficult paddling against both the wind and the tide.

We have paddled this route countless times—it is only about a mile from where we live in Portsmouth. There is nothing dramatic about the trek, and it never leaves civilization very far behind. Yet it is a wonderful trip, especially in summer when the wildlife returns to the area in large numbers—common terns, great blue herons, snowy egrets, and double-crested cormorants are almost guaranteed in midsummer. There is also a chance you will see white-tailed deer, harbor seals, and kingfishers, as well as the occasional red fox or red-tailed hawk. To top it off, you will paddle past a couple of historic buildings.

The sun shines down on the buildings of Portsmouth.

From the put-in on Pierce Island, paddle left. (Paddling right into the main channel of the Piscataqua is a dicey and sometimes dangerous proposition due to the very, very forceful tidal currents.) Paddle past Little Island and aim for the US 1B bridge that spans the channel between the mainland and Shapleigh Island. There is generally less current here than in the channel farther east. Once beyond this bridge, you are in an area of protected water with the island of New Castle to the east and Portsmouth and Rye to the west. Between are several smaller islands, with a larger, uninhabited, and wooded island in the middle of it all. For this trip, travel clockwise around the big island, known as Leach's Island. To do this, take a left after Shapleigh Island and then parallel US 1B, exploring the small islands until you reach New Castle. Turn right and follow the empty spaces between New Castle, Pest, and Leach's Islands.

As you round Leach's Island, you will see what remains of Wentworth-By-The-Sea, one of New Hampshire's old grand hotels built in the late eighteenth century. The Wentworth's claim to fame is that it was the site of the signing of the Treaty of Portsmouth in

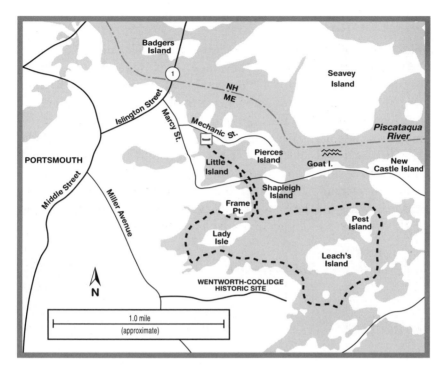

PORTSMOUTH HARBOR

1905. President Theodore Roosevelt negotiated this treaty, which ended a brutal war between Russia and Japan. The hotel has been closed since 1982, but there are currently plans to renovate and reopen it. To the left of the Wentworth is a narrow channel (strong current between tides) that leads under US 1B to Little Harbor and the open Atlantic. Instead of paddling under this bridge, continue past it toward Sagamore Creek. If you want to extend your trip, you can paddle up this creek for about 1.5 miles before you are stopped by salt marsh or mud flats, depending on the tide.

As you round Leach's Island, you will see the historic Wentworth Coolidge Mansion on the Portsmouth shore on your left. Built in 1741, this was the home of Benning Wentworth, the first royal governor of New Hampshire. On your right is the wooded shore of Leach's Island, which is surrounded by mud flats and salt marsh and is rich in bird life. You are now pointing back toward Pierce Island, heading north-northeast. At this point, you can either paddle back to the put-in, or take a left and paddle around Lady Isle, where you will find more woods, marsh, and wildlife-watching opportunities.

Directions

Take Exit 5 off I-95 to the Portsmouth traffic circle, and follow signs for Portsmouth and Woodbury Avenue. Turn right onto Woodbury Avenue and follow it to a T-intersection, where you turn right onto Bartlett Street, following signs for downtown Portsmouth. In another 0.2 mile, turn left at the light onto Islington Street. In another 0.6 mile, turn right at the light onto Middle Street. Pass through the light at State Street and take the next left onto Court Street. Go straight through two stop signs, then turn right onto Marcy Street when Court Street ends. In another 0.2 mile, turn left onto Mechanic Street. Parking for the Pierce Island boat launch is another 0.2 mile on the right. A parking fee is charged in summer.

Great Bay

> Difficulty: **Easy to Strenuous**
>
> Distance: **Various**
>
> Time: **1 hour to all day**
>
> Maps: **USGS Portsmouth and Newmarket Quadrangles and Maptech's Waterproof Chart #27**
>
> **A paddle along wooded shorelines and marshes with excellent wildlife–watching opportunities.**

WEATHER AND TIDE CONSIDERATIONS: Paddling during the hours around high tide makes this an easier trip. At low tide, you will be confined to a narrow channel that meanders through mud flats. Between tides, you will encounter strong currents that are difficult to paddle against. Winds of 10 knots and stronger can complicate matters, as Great Bay is a big, wide-open, shallow body of water. If you see whitecaps, stick close to shore or consider returning on another day.

While Great Bay is more than 13 miles upstream from the Atlantic Ocean, it is highly influenced by the changing tides: it is almost twice as large at high tide as it is at low. The Winnnicut, Squamscott, and Lamprey Rivers all empty into Great Bay, adding a large quantity of fresh water into this unique inland tidal ecosystem every day. The habitat of Great Bay provides rich feeding opportunities for a variety of wildlife, including more than 250 species of birds. The ecological significance of the bay is important enough that the federal government has established the Great Bay National Estuarine Research Reserve and the Great Bay National Wildlife Refuge within the last twenty years. While some housing developments have been constructed on the bay in recent years, there is still a big

Canoeing is a great way to explore New Hampshire's inland tidal waters.

chunk of undeveloped, shoreline worth exploring from one of the four put-ins we have listed below. Facilities are available only at Sandy Point.

Figuring out the tide situation is probably the most important piece of preparation for this trip, because mud flats can make it hard to get from your put-in to the water or vice versa, especially from the Sandy Point put-in. Some tide charts list information for the Squamscott River in Newfields—this is the best data to use for Great Bay. If you cannot find this information, expect the tides in Great Bay to run between 2 and 2^1/2 hours behind the tides in Portsmouth Harbor. If you intend to put in at Adams Point, plan to start your trip with the incoming tide and to finish it when the tide is slack or on its way out. The narrow channel between Adams Point and the Great Bay National Wildlife Refuge has to funnel all of the water that flows in and out of Great Bay, which means its current is very strong when the tide is changing.

We have not outlined a specific route for this trip—there are just too many possibilities. Whether you put in at Adams Point, Sandy Point, or Chapman's Landing, you can paddle for as long as you want. Some notable places to explore include the shoreline at the Great Bay Wildlife Refuge (including Woodman Point and Thomas Point), the Crommet Creek area near Adams Point, and the salt marshes and mud flats from Sandy Point to the mouth of the Squamscott River. From Chapman's Landing, you can also paddle up the Squamscott River for about 5.0 miles to downtown Exeter. No matter where you paddle, you are almost guaranteed to see a diversity of bird life, which varies from season to season. This variety includes wading birds like great blue herons, green herons, snowy egrets, great egrets, and glossy ibis, as well as about twenty-five species of shorebirds and an even larger variety of ducks and geese. Ospreys nest near the water; Great Bay is also home to the largest winter concentration of bald eagles in the state.

If you have kids in tow, visit the Sandy Point Discovery Center near the put-in at Sandy Point. This is an environmental education center with interpretive exhibits that include an estuarine touch tank and a model of Great Bay's tides. There are also a couple of miles of hiking trails that wind their way through oak-hickory forest and overlook the mud flats. In addition, there are good hiking trails at Adams Point, which is part of the Great Bay National Estuarine Reserve, and at Great Bay National Wildlife Refuge. (For directions, see the "Flat and Easy Walks" section in chapter 4.)

Directions to Sandy Point Put-In

From the intersection of NH 108 and NH 33 in Stratham, head east on NH 33. In 1.7 miles, turn left onto Depot Road, following the sign for the Sandy Point Discovery Center. In another 0.9 mile, turn left at a stop sign. The Discovery Center is on the left in about 0.1 mile, while the put-in is straight ahead in about 0.2 mile.

Directions to Chapman's Landing Put-In

Chapman's Landing is on the east side of NH 108 on the right bank of the Squamscott River, 0.3 mile south of NH 85, and 1.2 miles north of NH 33.

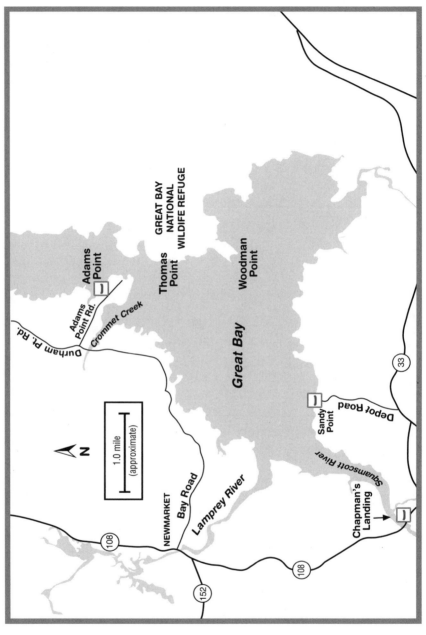

GREAT BAY

Directions to Adams Point Put-In

From the south: From the intersection of NH 108 and NH 152 in Newmarket, head north on NH 108. In 0.4 mile, just after crossing the Lamprey River, turn right onto Bay Road. In 3.8 miles, just after crossing Crommet Creek, turn right onto Adams Point Road. The boat launch is on the left in 0.9 mile.

From the north: From NH 108 in downtown Durham, follow NH 108 south for about 0.5 mile, where you turn left onto Durham Point Road. In 3.6 miles, turn left onto Adams Point Road and follow it to the boat launch.

Great Bay—
An Ecological Treasure

WITH MORE THAN 4,000 ACRES of tidal waters and 48 miles of shoreline at high tide, Great Bay provides plenty of paddling opportunities, but it is the bay's ecological significance that has attracted the most attention. Great Bay and its smaller neighbor Little Bay are a huge estuary where fresh water from seven rivers mixes with salt water that comes in on the tides from the Atlantic Ocean, 15 miles away. The bay is also very shallow—half of it is mud flats at low tide. The stirring of cold ocean water and warmer river water in the shallow bay creates a rich mix of nutrients that supports a wide variety of life, including oysters, horseshoe crabs, white-tailed deer, and bald eagles. The ecological significance of the bay has been recognized by the creation of the Great Bay National Estuarine Research Reserve, the Great Bay National Wildlife Refuge, Adams Point Wildlife Management Area, and smaller preserves owned by The Nature Conservancy.

Great Bay's earliest inhabitants were Abenaki Indians, who spent the warmer months of the year living next to the bay, fishing, hunting, and growing corn. Their kitchen middens, basically garbage piles of oyster- and clamshells and other artifacts, can still be found in various sites around the bay. The early American colonists recognized the bounty of the bay as well, harvesting oysters and salt marsh hay, which they hauled upriver in flat-bottomed boats called gundalows that were designed especially for travel in the Great Bay watershed. The bay was later home to dairy farms and orchards, which were eventually abandoned like many farms in New Hampshire. Now the shorelines of Great Bay are primarily forested.

Grommet Creek enters Great Bay at Adams Point.

While the bay is relatively clean today, it went through a period of moderate pollution from the late nineteenth through the mid-twentieth centuries as tanneries and textile mills released chemicals into the rivers upstream from the bay. Just as the watershed was beginning to recover from this pollution, the town of Durham successfully fought off an attempt to build a huge oil refinery complex on the bay and the offshore Isles of Shoals. If that project had been completed, the bay never would have recovered to the productive state it enjoys today. According to the National Oceanic and Atmospheric Administration, the biggest threat to the bay currently is bacterial contamination, stormwater, on-site sewage disposal systems, agricultural runoff, and runoff from shoreline development. This threat is relatively minor, although it has caused the closing of the bay's oyster beds in recent years.

What can you expect to see while paddling Great Bay? The habitats you will encounter include open water, tidal mud flats, salt marshes, creeks, rivers, and oak-hickory forests with tall white pines on the shorelines, often sitting atop rocky bluffs. Raccoon, red fox, and white-tailed deer are often seen on the shoreline; harbor seals fish in the water during high tide. It is the bird life, however, that draws most wildlife watchers to the bay. A checklist of Great Bay birds includes more than 250 species seen on the bay at some point during the year. A variety of herons, egrets, and shorebirds such as dowitchers and yellowlegs can usually be found feeding in the salt marshes and on the tidal flats. Most of the state's endangered and threatened bird species use the bay, including the common loon, pied-billed grebe, bald eagle, peregrine falcon, northern harrier, upland sandpiper, and common tern. Migrating waterfowl depend on the bay as well; it is common during migration time to see greater and lesser scaup, red-breasted merganser, Canada goose, golden-eye, brant, black duck, and oldsquaw.

To see the best of Great Bay, you need to paddle it over and over again and search out the special places that change from season to season and even day to day. As the tides move in and out and the seasons change, the animals of the bay change as well. One day you may see hundreds of water-fowl on the bay, while the next day the water may seem empty—but bald eagles will be soaring overhead. To get a truly complete picture of the bay, you should also walk the woodland paths at Adams Point, Sandy Point, and at the Great Bay National Wildlife Refuge, where coyotes hunt, woodcocks nest, and wild turkeys roam the oak-hickory forests.

Rye to Portsmouth

Difficulty: Moderate

Distance: 6.5 miles one-way

Time: 2¹/2 hours

Maps: USGS Kittery (Maine) Quadrangle, Maptech's Waterproof Chart #27

A scenic paddle along the rocky New Hampshire coast.

WEATHER AND TIDE CONSIDERATIONS: This trip is exposed to the full force of the Atlantic for much of its length. This stretch of coast is often exposed to large swells, and a windy day can make travel difficult, especially when winds are out of the northeast. Also, try to time the Little Harbor segment of your paddle with the incoming tide, as the current under the two US 1B bridges can be difficult to paddle against when the tide is going out.

This trip explores the quiet stretch of the New Hampshire coast north of the hustle and bustle of Hampton Beach. Starting near Rye Harbor, you will paddle past large rock ledges, cobble beaches, and the sands of Wallis Sands State Park. After rounding historic Odiorne Point, you will make your way through Little Harbor and the protected inner waters between New Castle and Portsmouth. The ocean views are spectacular, with the Isles of Shoals standing guard 6 miles offshore, and there is the chance to see interesting wildlife like harbor seals and seabirds. Restrooms are available at the put-in.

Put in on the north side of the parking area (not the harbor side) at Rye Harbor State Park, and paddle north-northeast along the shoreline, which consists of rock ledges and cobble beaches. If there are big swells, stay a good distance from shore—there are large rocks and submerged ledges near shore that need to be avoided. After

Cobblestones at Wallis Sands State Park.

about 1.5 miles, you will round Concord Point and see the long sandy beach of Wallis Sands State Park. Landing a boat on the state beach, at the southern and northern ends of the beach, is not allowed, but you can beach yourself and your boat by staying in the 100-yard section of beach just south of the breakwater. Just take care to be respectful of the local residents who own the property above the high-tide mark.

Immediately to the north of the beach are some tall rock ledges made of schist created during the Acadian Orogeny some 350 million years ago. These ledges also have some wide basalt dikes, layers of dark basalt that intruded into the schist as molten magma rose up from the separating layers of the earth's crust when the Pangea supercontinent broke apart. About 100 yards offshore from these ledges are a group of ledges known as Seal Rocks. It is common to see harbor seals hauled out on these rocks during low tide in spring and fall. Please view the seals from a distance with binoculars in order not to scare them into the water.

Just north of Seal Rocks lies Pulpit Rock, a popular spot for birders looking for sea ducks and purple sandpipers. Beyond Pulpit

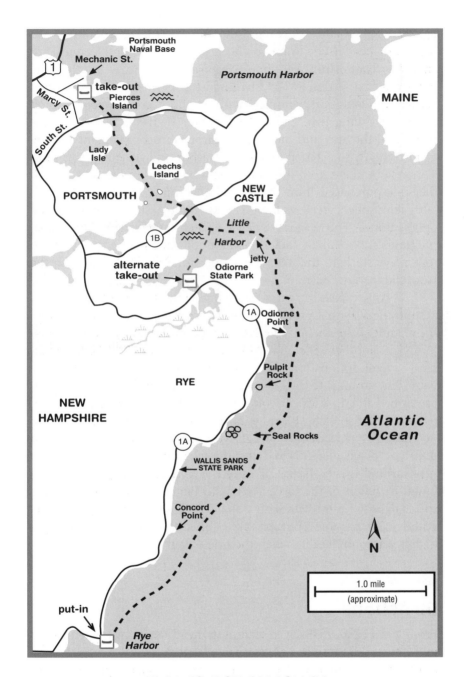

RYE TO PORTSMOUTH

Rock are two shallow coves and then a deeper cove where you can land your boat if you want to check out Odiorne Point State Park and New Hampshire Audubon's Seacoast Science Center. Odiorne Point was first settled in 1632 by English fishermen who established Pannaway Plantation, complete with a smithy, cooperage, fort, and stages for drying fish. During World War II, the U.S. government purchased the area and built Fort Dearborn to complement a string of forts that protected Portsmouth Harbor and its naval shipyard. Concrete bunkers from this era can still be found in the park, which the state purchased from the federal government in 1961. Now its 330 acres offer great walking, cross-country skiing, and birding opportunities. The Seacoast Science Center has excellent educational programs and exhibits, including an indoor tide pool where you can touch live starfish, urchins, crabs, and other shellfish native to the New Hampshire coast.

As you pass the varied shoreline of the state park, make a left around the jetty that protects Little Harbor from ocean swells. Across the channel from the jetty lie New Castle Island and Fort Stark Historic Site, another relic of World War II. Once in Little Harbor, you have several options for exploration. One is to follow the shore on your left around to Seavey Creek and its bird-rich salt marsh (described in trip #36). If you opt to continue toward Portsmouth, paddle under the US 1B bridge next to the Wentworth Hotel. Once on the other side of this bridge, you can either continue straight until you reach Pierce Island and the take-out or you can take side trips around Leachs Island or Lady Isle as described in trip #37. At low tide, much of the Little Harbor to Pierce Island section of this trip is exposed mud flats with a shallow channel running down the middle. Try to time your paddle of this section to coincide with higher water, preferably when the tide is high or rising.

Directions

From NH 111 and US 1A in Hampton, head north on US 1A. In 3.8 miles, turn right into Rye Harbor State Park. A parking fee is charged during the summer, and the parking area is open from 8 A.M. to 6 P.M. For directions for take-out on Pierce Island, see trip #37, p. 204.

The Isles of Shoals

SIX MILES OFF THE COAST OF RYE are the nine islands (north to south: Duck, Appledore, Malaga, Smuttynose, Cedar, Star, Luning, White, and Seavy) that comprise the Isles of Shoals, small hills that rise from the bottom of the Atlantic just enough to create a little dry land. The islands range in size from a few acres to the relatively spacious ninety-five acres on Appledore Island, and are easily visible from the mainland on a clear day. Politically, the islands are divided between Maine and New Hampshire, but geologically they are part of the Rye formation, a durable metamorphic schist that withstood the erosive power of the glaciers as they dug out the deep waters surrounding the islands.

These waters were discovered early on by European fishermen, and by the eighteenth century, there were as many as 600 people living on the islands. Most residents left the Isles of Shoals during the Revolutionary War because the colonies could not guarantee them protection from the British. Currently, there are no full-time residents of the islands, although there are a few summer homes as well as a marine research facility run by Cornell and the University of New Hampshire, a lighthouse, and the Oceanic Hotel, which hosts summer conferences. Day-trippers can visit Star and Appledore Islands by taking a cruise with the Isles of Shoals Steamship Company from Portsmouth (603-431-5500).

The Isles of Shoals were one of New Hampshire's biggest tourist attractions in the 1800s, when the Oceanic and the Appledore Hotels attracted Boston's elite for lengthy stays in the cool ocean air. The natural allure of the islands was complemented by the poetry of Celia Thaxter and mysterious stories about shipwrecked Spanish fishermen and tales of pirates' treasure. (Blackbeard reportedly left his thirteenth wife on Lunging Island—did he leave gold and silver as well?) Recently the islands have reappeared in the world of literature in Anita Shreve's novel *The Weight of Water*, which delves into the real-life mystery of an ax murder that occurred on Smuttynose Island in 1873, and *Island Queen: Celia Thaxter of Isles of Shoals*, a historical fiction novel by Julia Older.

On occasion local outfitters lead sea kayaking trips to the isles, where they transport you and your boat to the islands before you start paddling. It is possible to kayak to the islands from the mainland, but it is a very long, difficult paddle that requires a great deal of experience and knowledge of local ocean tides and currents.

Squam Lake

> Difficulty: **Easy to Strenuous**
>
> Distance: **Various**
>
> Time: **1 hour to 3 days**
>
> Maps: **USGS Holderness, Squam Mountains, and Center Sandwich Quadrangles**
>
> **Classic Lakes Region paddling—loons, mountain views, and wooded islands with camping opportunities.**

SQUAM LAKE IS THE KINDER, northern neighbor of Lake Winnipesaukee. That is not to say this 6,700-plus-acre lake is free of development and boat traffic—much of the shore is well developed and there are plenty of motorboats and Jet Skis, especially on summer weekends. Nonetheless, there are still pristine stretches of wooded shoreline that give the lake a wild feeling, especially when you gaze up at the surrounding mountains and listen to the calls of common loons. Because Squam is such a big lake, we have included it in this chapter because it is ideal for sea kayaks, although it is also a good place to load up a canoe with the family for the day or an overnight camping trip. The large size of the lake does make it prone to dangerous waves in windy conditions—keep an eye on the weather and be prepared for quickly changing conditions. Lightning strikes are also a real possibility during the summer thunderstorm season.

You really can paddle for as long as you want on Squam Lake—there is enough shoreline to keep you occupied for several days. One popular trip is to head out to Moon and Bowman Islands in the center of the lake and take advantage of the public access there for a picnic and quick swim. It can be completed in two or three

The northern end of Squam lake as seen from Eagle Cliff.

hours from any of the three put-ins described below, with the Pipers Cove put-in providing the closest access. Moon and Bowman Islands are owned by the Squam Lakes Association (SLA), which maintains hiking trails and campsites on the islands that are open to public use. The SLA also maintains campsites in the Chamberlain Reynolds Memorial Forest, which is adjacent to Dog Cove. If you want to spend the night, make reservations ahead of time. More information is available from the SLA at P.O. Box 204, Holderness, NH 03245, 603-968-7336, www.squamlakes.org.

In addition to the SLA properties and the Chamberlain Reynolds forest, there is public access (though no camping) at the University of New Hampshire's property at Five Fingers Point at the northern end of the lake below the Rattlesnake Hills. At Five Fingers Point, there are coves and wooded shoreline to explore as well as sandy beaches and trails up to the views from the Rattlesnakes. (Look for the trail in True Cove.) Except for these preserves that are open to the public, the rest of the shoreline on Squam Lake is private property—try to plan your break needs for the above points of public access. Pit toilets are located on the SLA properties.

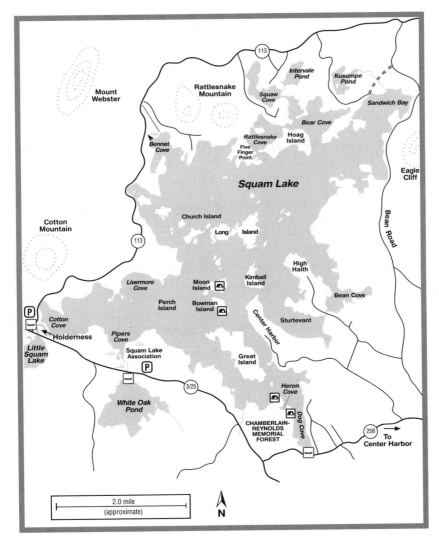

SQUAM LAKE

One of the appeals of Squam Lake is its status as a stronghold of the common loon; recent years have seen more than twenty nesting pairs of loons here. You will most likely encounter loons during your paddle, and it is important to give them a wide berth to avoid disturbing them, especially during nesting season in spring and early summer. Several coves in the lake that are home to loon nests are marked off-limits to boats during the nesting season, and this includes canoes and kayaks. Enjoy the beauty of Squam's loons through your binoculars and your ears—their calls are one of the most beautiful sounds heard in southern New Hampshire.

Directions to Holderness Put-In

Boat access is on the south side of NH 113, just east of NH 25 and US 3 in Holderness.

Directions to Pipers Cove Put-In

From US 3 and NH 113 in Holderness, head south on US 3. The put-in is at the Squam Lakes Association Headquarters in Pipers Cove on the right in 1.5 miles.

Directions to Dog Cove Put-In

From NH 25 and NH 25B in Center Harbor, head west on NH 25B. The put-in is at the tip of Dog Cove on the right side of the road about 2.2 miles from Center Harbor. There is a 200-foot carry to the water.

8
river trips

SOUTHERN NEW HAMPSHIRE is blessed with numerous navigable rivers. This chapter looks at ten of those rivers, from the narrow, creeklike Nissitissit to the broad, slow-moving waters of the upper Connecticut. Some of these trips are easy flatwater paddles, while others are exhilarating whitewater runs, although we have chosen sections of rivers with a maximum rating of Class II. (Experienced paddlers looking to run Class III and higher whitewater should check out the AMC's *Classic Northeastern Whitewater Guide* by Bruce Lessels, which explains in great detail the best whitewater in the Northeast.) All of these trips require varying levels of experience on fast-moving water. Please read this introduction and the trip descriptions in detail before deciding if you have the skills necessary to safely complete a trip. River paddling is extremely rewarding, but it also a very dangerous sport to participate in without the proper training.

Gauges

For some of the river trips in this chapter, we list gauge readings that can be checked as a way to determine the conditions on a river. Gauges can be simple lines painted on a bridge abutment that mark the stage (usually measured in feet) of a river. We also mention USGS gauges that measure both stage and river flow. River flow is measured by cubic feet per second (CFS,) or the amount of water that flows by the gauge in one second. The USGS gauges can be accessed on the internet through the AWA's website as well as the USGS website http//:water.usgs.gov/realtime.html. Not all rivers have these gauges, and you need to use your group's experience and best judgement when determining whether a river is at a safe level.

River Ratings

The river ratings we use in this book are based on the American version of the international scale of difficulty as described by the American Whitewater Affiliation. American Whitewater has an excellent website for learning about boating safety and river conservation: www.americanwhitewater.org.

- Class I: Easy. Fast moving water with riffles and small waves. Few obstructions, all obvious and easily missed with little training. Risk to swimmers is slight; self-rescue is easy.

- Class II: Novice. Straightforward rapids with wide, clear channels that are evident without scouting. Occasional maneuvering may be required, but rocks and medium-sized waves are easily missed by trained paddlers. Swimmers are seldom injured and group assistance, while helpful, is seldom needed.

- Class III: Intermediate. Rapids with moderate, irregular waves that may be difficult to avoid and that can swamp an open canoe. Complex maneuvers in fast current and good boat control are often required; large waves or strainers may be present but are easily avoided. Strong eddies and powerful current effects can be found, particularly on large-volume rivers. Scouting is advisable for inexperienced parties. Injuries while swimming are rare; self-rescue is usually easy, but group assistance may be required to avoid long swims.

- Class IV: Advanced. Intense, powerful but predictable rapids requiring precise boat handling in turbulent water. Depending on the character of the river, it may feature large, unavoidable waves and holes or constricted passages demanding fast maneuvers under pressure. A fast, reliable eddy turn may be needed to initiate maneuvers, scout rapids, or rest. Rapids may require "must" moves above dangerous hazards. Scouting is necessary the first time down. Risk of injury to swimmers is moderate to high, and water conditions may make self-rescue difficult. Group assistance for rescue is often essential but requires practiced skills. A strong Eskimo roll is highly recommended.

- Class V: Expert. Extremely long, obstructed, or very violent rapids that expose a paddler to above average endangerment. Drops may contain large, unavoidable waves and holes and steep, congested chutes with complex, demanding routes. Rapids may continue for long distances between pools, demanding a high level of fitness. What eddies exist may be small, turbulent, or difficult to reach. At the high end of the scale, several of these factors may be combined. Scouting is mandatory but often difficult even for experts. A very reliable Eskimo roll, proper equipment, extensive experience, and practiced rescue skills are essential for survival.

- Class VI: Extreme. One grade more difficult than Class V. These runs often exemplify the extremes of difficulty, unpredictability, and danger. The consequences of error are severe and rescue may be impossible. For teams of experts only, at favorable water levels, after close personal inspection and taking all precautions. This class does not represent drops thought to be unrunnable, but may include rapids that are only occasionally run.

Safety

Following these guidelines can save your life:

- Never paddle alone. The American Whitewater Affiliation (www.americanwhitewater.org) recommends paddling with at least three people and two boats. The AMC suggests three boats.

- Dress for the water temperature. Water temperatures in spring are often in the thirties and forties. Immersion in water this cold (or even as warm as sixty degrees) is a shock to your system that can cause an involuntary gasp reflex that can hinder your ability to deal with hazards in the water. The body loses heat very rapidly in water, and hypothermia is a very real risk after an accidental swim. If a member of your group becomes clumsy, slurs speech, or begins to shiver, get him or her into warm dry clothes immediately and offer warm fluids and food. Dress in layers and stay well fed in order to prevent hypothermia. Wear a polypro of silk wicking layers close to your body, followed by wool or fleece, and topped by a wet or dry suit. Do not wear cotton as it absorbs water and has no insulating properties when wet. Also wear neoprene paddling gloves and a wool or polypro hat under your helmet. Pack extra clothes in a dry bag to change into in case you get wet.

- Always wear a Coast Guard–approved personal flotation device (PFD), even when scouting a river. Make sure your PFD is rated for turbulent water and that it allows freedom of movement for swimming and paddling.

- Boaters in kayaks or closed canoes should always wear a helmet—you *will* at some point hit your head on a rock while upside down in your boat. Open-boaters should wear helmets in rapids that are rated Class II and higher.

- Outfit your boat with flotation so that it will still float if it gets swamped.

- Make sure you and your boat are outfitted in such a way that nothing can get tangled or hooked on the branches of fallen trees or other obstacles in the river. People drown because they get caught underwater on trees that have fallen into the river.

- Never stand up in whitewater. The power of whitewater should not be underestimated. Standing up puts you at risk for getting a foot caught between rocks on the bottom of the river. Once this happens, the force of the water can force you underwater—you can drown in less than 2 feet of water.

- Be practiced in self-rescue. Do *not* get into a boat on moving water if you have not previously practiced escape from your boat. This is especially important for kayakers, who must be able to wet-exit their boat in case they flip.

- Know how to use your boat in moving water. If you have never paddled on whitewater, you should take a course in whitewater techniques. Many of these techniques will help you not only enjoy your trip, but also avoid life-threatening situations. After some basic training, all of the trips in this book are appropriate for beginning paddlers who are paddling with a group of experienced whitewater paddlers. The AMC's New Hampshire Chapter has a whitewater school in southern New Hampshire every spring that provides excellent training. The AMC has also started whitewater training workshops at Pinkham Notch in the White Mountains.

- While moving downstream, always stay between the lead and sweep boats, and keep the boat behind you in sight.

- Learn to recognize and avoid these whitewater hazards:

High water: The more water in a river, the more powerful and dangerous it is. Do not attempt to paddle a river at or near flood stage. While we have given some guidelines to gauge each river by, we have not paddled these rivers in all conditions, and you must use your own judgment in determining the safety of a river's water level. Also, streambeds can change, making our gauge recommendations obsolete. If you are unsure of a river's safety, check with the forest service or local outfitters. Be aware that rivers can rise and fall considerably during the course of a few hours due to runoff and snowmelt. The National Oceanic and Atmospheric Administration (NOAA) and National Weather Service publish current river flow data on the NOAA website: www.nws.noaa.gov/er/nerfc/gis_maps/. You can also use the U.S. Geological Survey (USGS) flow information at http://water.usgs.gov/realtime.html.

Strainers: Fallen trees and other obstacles through which water can flow, but not you and your boat, are called strainers. These are very dangerous: you can become pinned against the object, where you will be subject to immense water pressure. Rescue from these situations can be difficult or impossible. Learn to spot these obstacles well ahead of time, and be proficient enough to maneuver your boat around them.

Dams, ledges, reversals, holes, and hydraulics: Most of the holes and hydraulics encountered on the trips in this book are relatively benign. It is important, however, not to approach dams or strong holes from either direction; they can be impossible to escape in some circumstances.

Broaching: If your boat is pushed sideways against a rock by strong current, you run the risk of being pinned against the rock and crushed by the current. This is an especially dangerous situation for kayakers, who can get trapped in their boat with no way to escape. To avoid being pinned in this situation, throw your weight downstream, even going so far as to lean against the rock. This will allow the current to flow harmlessly under your boat.

To safely paddle whitewater, everyone in your group should have rudimentary paddling skills. Kayakers should know how to use the following strokes/techniques: forward stroke, sweep, reverse sweep, draw, high brace, low brace. They should also be able to safely exit a flipped boat and swim to safety. Canoeists should know how to use the following strokes: forward stroke, J stroke, backstroke, draw, cross draw, forward sweep, reverse sweep, low brace, and high brace. All boaters should know how to ferry, back ferry, and how to safely enter and exit an eddy. If any of these strokes/techniques are unfamiliar to you, get some training before risking your life on the river.

For additional safety and a more comfortable trip, bring the following:

Water—one or more quarts per person, depending on the weather and length of the trip

Food—even for a one-hour trip, it is a good idea to bring some high-energy snacks such as nuts, dried fruit, or snack bars; bring a lunch for longer trips.

Map and compass

Extra clothing to warm up in after immersion in cold water

Flashlight

Sunscreen

First-aid kit

Pocketknife

Spare paddle

Etiquette and the Environment

- Like all outdoor sports, river paddling requires that we all follow Leave No Trace techniques (see chapter 1) in order to prevent environmental degradation and preserve the wilderness experience for those who follow us. Take great care when walking on shore—the environment along the riverbanks can be especially fragile. Also, all of the river trips in this book pass through private property for most of their length, so please treat the environment with care and act with courtesy.

- If you are part of an especially large group (more than twelve boats), break your trip into two or more groups in order to relieve congestion.

- Get in and out of the water quickly—others may be waiting to use the put-in or take-out.

- Don't peel out in front of another boat.

- Don't hog eddies, surfing waves, or holes. Get your rest and have your fun, but others probably want to use the same river features you are enjoying.

- If you swim, use self-rescue skills as much as possible.

Local Paddling Groups

Joining a paddling club is a great way to enjoy whitewater safely. There are many clubs in New England. In New Hampshire the following groups are always willing to take on enthusiastic new paddlers:

- AMC New Hampshire Paddlers: AMC members can join this group by contacting the paddling co-chair. (Check the "Chapter Activities" section of AMC Outdoors for a current listing.) Visit www.nhamcpaddlers.org/.

- Merrimack Valley Paddlers: P.O. Box 233, Hollis, NH 03049, www.mvpclub.org/.

You are trained, you are equipped, you are ready to paddle. The trips in this chapter will take you through historic mill towns and provide encounters with animals such as minks, otters, ospreys, and bald eagles. They will also throw whitewater challenges at you that will make it impossible to pay any attention to wildlife on shore or overhead. You will find rock gardens and surfing waves and even a few holes in which to throw your play boat. We'll see you on the river.

Contoocook River

Difficulty: Easy flat water in low water; strong, pushy quick water in high water

Distance: 7.0 miles

Estimated Time: 3^1/$_2$ hours

Maps: USGS Hopkinton Quadrangle

An easy half–day paddle through the New Hampshire countryside.

THE CONTOOCOOK IS ONE OF NEW HAMPSHIRE'S high-volume rivers, beginning near the Massachusetts border in Jaffrey and flowing north to enter the Merrimack River in Concord. The "Took" is well known to whitewater paddlers for an exciting Class IV run of rapids called Freight Train, followed up by S-Turn in Henniker. In contrast, the section of the river described in this trip is a placid flatwater paddle in the village of Contoocook that flows past farms and is bordered by floodplains covered in beautiful forests of silver maples. While this is usually an easy paddle, it can be tricky or even dangerous in high water—the current gets very turbulent and pushy, requiring you to use the paddling skills outlined in the introduction to this chapter. The best time to run this river is in fall, when the current is negligible and the trees are ablaze in color. No facilities are available in the area.

From the put-in, the river flows past farms above high banks lined with tall maples and oaks. After about 1.5 miles, you begin to see a few houses. At 2.5 miles, pass under a bridge next to Rattlesnake Hill where timber was cut for the USS *Kearsarge*, a Civil War battleship built in Portsmouth that sank the Confederate ship *Alabama* in a decisive battle off the French coast. After the bridge, there are more farms with white pines on the high banks. Low-lying

A fall day on the Contoocook River.

areas are covered in silver maples whose graceful arching branches hang over the river. One of the nicest stands of silver maple is on a large island in the center of the river about 4.5 miles from the put-in. At 5.2 miles, you pass under a set of power lines and past an old bridge abutment, but the river is already taking on a decidedly woodsy feel, with white pines and northern hardwoods making up the forest beyond the high banks.

After a long section without houses, the river will bend to the left where a house sits high up on the right bank. Just before this house is the marshy Broad Cove on the right. Head into this cove to reach the take-out.

Directions to Put–In

Take Exit 6 off I-89 and head north on NH 127. In about 1.3 miles, you reach a T-intersection with NH 103 in the center of Contoocook. Drive straight across this intersection into a parking lot behind a building next to the river. The put-in is below this parking lot.

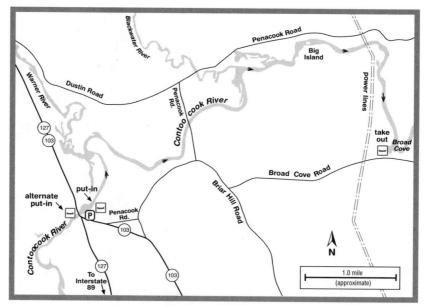

CONTOOCOOK

Alternate Put–In

This put-in is just upriver from the above put-in. It runs a short section of Class I rapids that can be fun in high water but are not runnable during low water. From the above-mentioned T-intersection, turn left onto NH 103. In about 100 yards, turn left onto the unnamed road just before the bridge. In another 100 yards there is a public parking area on the right with access to the river.

Directions to Take–Out

From the put-in, turn left out of the parking lot onto NH 103. In 0.3 mile, turn left onto Penacook Road. In another 0.4 mile, turn left at a stop sign to stay on Penacook Road. In another 1.0 mile, turn right onto Briar Hill Road. In 0.5 mile, turn left onto Broad Cove Road. Park in the pullout on the left in 1.8 miles. The take-out is in Broad Cove, about 100 yards below the pullout, down an old woods road.

Anadromous Fish

NEW HAMPSHIRE'S COASTAL RIVERS once teemed with runs of tens of thousands of Atlantic salmon, American shad, and other anadromous fish. Anadromous fish hatch in fresh water and spend the first few years of their lives there before migrating to the open ocean. After several years they return to the freshwater streams where they were born in

Salmon fry ready for release into the Lamprey River.

order to spawn. In addition to salmon and shad, other anadromous fish found in New Hampshire are rainbow smelt, striped bass, and river herring (alewife and blueback herring). Populations of anadromous fish dropped precipitously throughout New England in the late nineteenth century as a result of water pollution and dam construction. Now that New Hampshire rivers are much cleaner, some populations have returned, but dams still prevent many fish from reaching their spawning grounds. Dams also cause problems upstream, as they cause water to warm up to temperatures unsuitable for some fish. And they can cause silt to build up, covering spawning beds.

The hardest-hit fish were Atlantic salmon and shortnose sturgeon, and to a lesser extent American shad and river herring. The state of New Hampshire is working to increase shad and river herring numbers by trapping and relocating spawning adults from other New England rivers and releasing them in New Hampshire. There are no longer "wild" runs of Atlantic salmon in New Hampshire; these fish now only occur in Canada and a few rivers in eastern Maine. The state does release salmon fry on the Lamprey and Cocheco Rivers in the hope they will return to spawn in four to six years. How well this will all work is still to be seen. Anadromous fish are very finely programmed to spawn in their native rivers and streams; scientists are not sure if relocating fish and using stock fish will result in a naturally reproducing population.

Connecticut River

Difficulty: Flat water

Distance: 13.5 miles, with a shorter 5.7–mile option

Estimated Time: 6 hours

Maps: USGS Fairlee (Vermont) and Lyme Quadrangles

A flatwater paddle past farms and wooded hillsides on New England's largest river.

THE CONNECTICUT RIVER is New England's longest, flowing more than 400 miles from New Hampshire's border with Quebec to Long Island Sound. The river starts as a small beaver pond in the Northern Forest, but it takes on several different characteristics on its journey south—rushing whitewater, meandering flat water, urban waterway, and tidal estuary. This trip explores 13-plus miles of the river north of Hanover, where the river backs up behind a dam, creating a long stretch of deep flat water bordered by farms and rolling hills. You do have to share the river with motorboats, but so do the swallows, kingfishers, and herons that you will see along the way. This is a long paddle that can seem even longer if there is a wind out of the south or southwest. Because there is relatively little current on this stretch of river, you can always complete a shorter out-and-back paddle from the put-in. We have also listed an alternative take-out that is only 5.7 miles from the put-in.

At the put-in, you might consider paddling upriver for 0.5 mile or so to look for peregrine falcons, which are once again nesting on the cliffs across the river in Fairlee, Vermont. After turning around and heading downstream, you will be in lazy river mode— there is no perceptible current. This is a great summer paddle when the water and the breezes are warm and the banks are abloom with

A covered bridge spans Clay Brook near its confluence with the Connecticut River.

Canada lilies and joe-pye weed. Not far from the put-in, you will pass some high sandy cliffs on river left (east) where swallows nest in the banks. We even saw a woodchuck peering from its den (probably a great staging ground for making raids on the nearby farm) high up on the cliff wall. After about 3.0 miles, Clay Brook enters the river from the left—a short paddle up this stream will bring you to a covered bridge over River Road.

About 1.0 mile past Clay Brook, a grassy picnic area and campsite on river right (west) makes a good lunch spot. This site and others along the river are on private property and are open to the

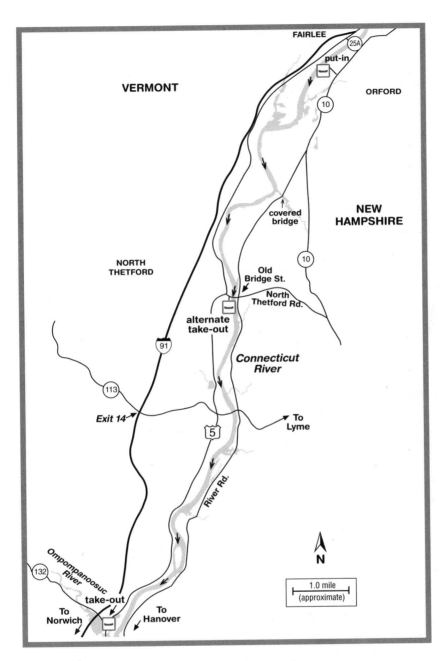

FAIRLEE

25A

put-in

VERMONT

ORFORD

10

covered
bridge

NEW
HAMPSHIRE

NORTH
THETFORD

Old
Bridge St.

10

North
Thetford Rd.

alternate
take-out

Connecticut
River

91

113

Exit 14

5

To
Lyme

River Rd.

N

1.0 mile
(approximate)

Ompompanoosuc
River

132

take-out

To
Norwich

To
Hanover

CONNECTICUT RIVER

public, but their status may change. The Upper Valley Land Trust (www.uvlt.org, 603-643-6626) maintains a current list of these sites and works to ensure public access. The river meanders past more farms and forest on its way to North Thetford, Vermont, where you will see a few houses. You pass the alternate take-out on the right in North Thetford as well. Below North Thetford is more of the same—big meandering flat water, embellished by fragrant water lilies, reeds, and cattails. Thirteen miles from the put-in, you will notice a railroad trestle on your right. Paddle under this trestle and head up the Ompompanoosuc River into Vermont. About 0.25 mile upriver after passing under US 5, you reach the take-out on the right.

Directions to Put–In

From the intersection of NH 25A and NH 10 in Orford, head south on NH 10. In about 100 yards, turn right onto Boat Landing Road. The put-in is at the end of this road in about 0.25 mile.

Directions to Take–Out

Head back to NH 10, turn left, and then left again onto NH 25A. Cross the river into Vermont and turn left onto US 5. In 7.6 miles, turn right onto Old Bridge Street. In about 150 yards, turn left into a dirt driveway that leads to the take-out on the Ompompanoosuc River.

Directions to Alternate Take–Out

Head back to NH 10, turn left, and then left again onto NH 25A. Cross the river into Vermont and turn left onto US 5. In 5.7 miles, turn left onto Bridge Road in North Thetford. The road crosses a set of railroad tracks then bends right and leads to the take-out.

Merrimack River— Franklin to Boscawen

> **Difficulty: Flat water and quick water with one short Class I section (Class II in high water)**
> **Distance: 6.3 miles, with longer options**
> **Estimated Time: 3 hours**
> **Maps: USGS Franklin and Webster Quadrangles**
>
> **An easy summer paddle on one of New Hampshire's best-known and largest rivers.**

THE MERRIMACK RIVER is born in Franklin at the confluence of the Pemigewasset and Winnipesaukee Rivers. It is best known as the river that powered the textile mills in Manchester, Lowell, and Lawrence during the past century. Terribly polluted just thirty years ago, the Merrimack is considerably cleaner today and supports populations of anadramous fish, which in turn attract herons, ospreys, and bald eagles. This trip begins on the Winnipesaukee River, just before it meets the Pemigewasset. The first 0.5 mile or so consists of easy Class I rapids (these can be tricky Class II in high water), but the remainder of the trip consists of quick water and flat water. This is a great trip in summer because it almost always has enough water to be passable.

This is a fairly scenic trip bordered by beautiful stands of hardwood forest. Great blue herons and kingfishers seem to be fishing on every mile of the river, while sandpipers flit about the shoreline eating insects. About 1.5 miles below the put-in, you pass a pair of very large granite bridge abutments that are all that remains of Franklin Junction. In the days of rail travel, this is where tourists changed trains to head either to the White Mountains or Montreal.

After Franklin Junction, the river makes a series of turns that are prone to strainers as the river undercuts its banks on the outside of the turns.

It is an easy paddle the rest of the way to the take-out as you pass tall red and white pines and a shoreline full of wildflowers such as irises, cardinal flowers, asters, and arrowroot. To extend your trip another 4.7 miles, keep paddling flat water until you reach the first alternate take-out described below. For a very long, 18.0-mile day, you can continue to the second alternate take-out, which comes after an additional 7.0 miles of flat water followed by a few hundred yards of Class II rapids (not shown on map).

Directions to Put–In

From Exit 20 off I-93, head south on US 3. After passing through the center of Franklin, turn left into the high school, about 5.0 miles from I-93. Follow signs for the boat ramp on the left, which is about 200 yards from US 3.

Directions to Take–Out

Drive back to US 3 and go south. In 0.3 mile, turn left at the light onto South Main Street in order to stay on US 3. In 5.8 miles, turn left onto a dirt road marked Merrimack County Boat Launching Facility. The take-out is at the end of the road.

Alternate Take–Out 1

Drive 3.8 miles south of the above take-out, turn left onto Depot Street, and follow it to the river, where you turn right and park next to the baseball fields.

Alternate Take–Out 2 (not shown on map)

From alternate take-out 1, continue south on US 3. In 0.9 mile, stay left at the fork and follow NH 4 east. In 3.1 miles, turn right onto NH 132. In another 1.1 miles, turn right onto Sewall Falls Road. In another 0.5 mile, turn left after crossing the river into the Sewalls Falls Multi-Use Recreation Area.

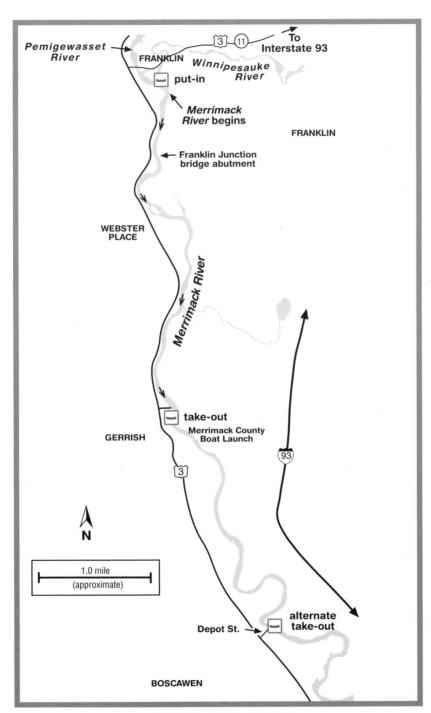

MERRIMACK RIVER

The Historic Merrimack

THE MERRIMACK BEGINS at the confluence of the Pemigewasset and Winnipesaukee Rivers in Franklin, New Hampshire, and flows 120 miles to the Atlantic Ocean in Newburyport, Massachusetts. Draining more than 5,000 square miles in the western White Mountains, the Lakes Region, most of central New Hampshire, and part of northern Massachusetts, the Merrimack watershed is the fourth largest in New England. The watershed has changed considerably since the end of the last ice age. As the ice retreated from the Merrimack Valley, the Merrimack and the Pemigewasset were both submerged under Lake Merrimack from Lowell, Massachusetts, all the way to Plymouth, New Hampshire. The lower part of the lake was brackish; seawater reached as far as Manchester. In the years following the retreat of the glacier, the land in the northern part of the valley rose about 400 feet as it was released from the weight of the ice. This new tilt to the land eventually drained the lake, leaving us with the river valley we see today.

Native Americans probably began living in the Merrimack Valley as soon as the ice melted and the lake drained. Several Native American archaeological sites have been found along the upper Merrimack, dating back 8,000 years. At the time of European contact, the Penacook tribe of Algonkians lived along the Merrimack, which was the center of Native American life in New Hampshire. With European settlement, the river became a major transportation route between the farming communities in the region. By the nineteenth century the Merrimack was one of the most important centers of commerce in the United States, with textile mills lining the banks in Lawrence, Lowell, Manchester, and Concord. The river was dammed and routed into canals to provide power and expedite transportation. The Sewell Falls Dam, built in the late 1800s in Concord, is the nation's oldest hydroelectric dam.

A floodplain forest next to the Merrimack River.

The dams and pollution associated with the mills decimated the anadromous fishery. Over the past thirty years the river has been cleaned up and fish ladders installed at dam sites, but most anadromous species are still at risk, especially shortnose sturgeon (a state and federally listed endangered species) and Atlantic salmon, which only exist here because the river is stocked with fish raised in hatcheries. Despite the problems with anadromous fish (which are having problems along the entire East Coast), the river supports a large and healthy variety of wildlife including river otters, ospreys, great blue herons, and bald eagles, which nested along the river for the first time in recent history in 2001. The river is also important habitat for rare and endangered species such as the Karner blue butterfly, Blanding's turtles, and brook floater mussels.

The river also supports a vibrant paddling community with nine public access points within New Hampshire. The Merrimack River paddling trip in this book explores a portion of the upper Merrimack, 30 miles of which was designated part of the New Hampshire Rivers Management and Protection Program in 1990. This designation was made because of the upper Merrimack's relatively undeveloped character—80 percent of the land within 0.75 mile of the upper Merrimack is undeveloped farm-, forest-, or wetland. This portion of the river sustains six ecologically significant habitats: floodplain forest, inland dunes, pine barrens, sandy river bluff forest, mesic river bluff forest, and an acidic riverside seep community. All of these habitat types are rare in New Hampshire, and pine barrens are considered a globally rare natural community. The significance of the upper Merrimack has been recognized by the National Park Service, which has identified it as eligible for inclusion in the National Wild and Scenic Rivers System.

The Merrimack River is in good shape today, although it still is threatened in the long run by sewer outflows, non-point-source pollution, loss of wetlands habitat, and increased demand for water. Fortunately, there are several organizations devoted to protecting the river, including the EPA, the New Hampshire Department of Environmental Services, and the Merrimack Watershed Council, which brings businesses, communities, and individuals together to find ways to protect the watershed. The council also leads paddling trips throughout the summer on the Merrimack and other rivers in the watershed. For more information, call 978-681-5777 or visit www.merrimack.org.

Nissitissit River

> Difficulty: **Quick water**
>
> Distance: **6.5 miles**
>
> Estimated Time: **4 hours**
>
> Maps: **USGS Townsend (Massachusetts) and Pepperell (Massachusetts) Quadrangles**
>
> **An early–spring paddle through scenic forests on a narrow quickwater river.**

THE NISSITISSIT IS A SMALL RIVER that begins at Potanipo Pond in Brookline and flows south to meet the Nashua River in Pepperell, Massachusetts. This trip explores about 6.5 of the river's 10 miles. Despite its diminutive size, the Nissitissit is a great river to paddle right after ice-out, when the rest of New Hampshire's rivers are still choked with ice. March and possibly early April are usually the only times there is enough water in the Nissitissit for paddling, which means you are often paddling when there is still snow on the banks. There are no rapids on this trip, but the river does move along at a quick pace, and its twisting nature creates the potential for encountering surprise strainers. Other than strainers, only the cold water of winter should concern you, so stay in your boat and be dressed to survive an accidental swim (see page 225). No facilities are nearby.

From the put-in, paddle past a few houses as you leave the center of Brookline then quickly enter the first of several marshy, meandering sections of river; you may encounter some of the first birds of spring here, such as red-winged blackbirds. After about 2.0 miles, the river continues its meandering ways, but instead of marsh, you are now paddling through a surprisingly undeveloped forest of hemlocks, oaks, and mountain laurel. The wooded shoreline shows

The Nissitissit River in early spring.

sign of beaver activity, and sharp eyes may spot a mink as it patrols the shoreline in search of food. After about 4.5 miles, you reach the Pepperell Road bridge and alternate take-out. This is also a good spot for lunch: you are on the land of the Beaver Brook Association, which protects nearly 2,000 acres of land in Brookline and Hollis.

The river continues to meander through relatively undeveloped forest for the final 2.0 miles to the take-out. Just prior to the take-out, look for an old dam that is runnable in high water—just pick a spot between the rocks. At the take-out, it is usually easier to take out on river left and carry your boat over the bridge back to the car.

Directions to Put-In

From the intersection of NH 130 and NH 13 north of Brookline, head east on NH 130. In 2.0 miles, turn right onto Meetinghouse Hill Road. In about 100 yards, turn left into the driveway between the Brookline police and fire stations. The put-in is behind the fire station, but park behind the police station.

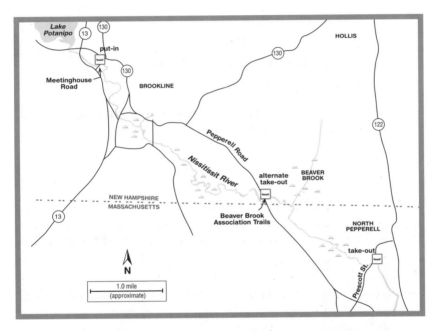

NISSITISSIT

Directions to Take-Out

Turn right out of the parking lot back onto Meetinghouse Hill Road. Take a right at the next two stop signs, which are within about 100 yards of the fire station. You are now back on NH 130 (Main Street), heading east. In 0.7 mile, stay left at the fork in the road. In another 1.0 mile, continue straight onto Pepperell Road as NH 130 turns left. In 1.6 miles, Pepperell Road crosses a bridge where there is a parking area for Beaver Brook Association Trails—this is an alternate take-out if you prefer a shorter trip. In another 2.0 miles, turn left onto Prescott Street. The take-out is on the left in another 0.4 mile, just before the bridge crosses the river.

Lamprey River

Difficulty: **Class II and flat water**

Distance: **7.0 miles**

Estimated Time: **3 hours**

Maps: **USGS Mount Pawtuckaway and Epping Quadrangles**

A diverse paddle on the longest river on the New Hampshire seacoast.

DURING THE COURSE OF ITS 60–MILE JOURNEY from Northwood to Newmarket, the Lamprey changes from a small rocky stream to a large tidal river. In between it alternates between slow meanders and rocky rapids, reaching Class III at Packers Falls in Durham. This trip explores 7.0 miles of this National Wild and Scenic River as it winds its way through Epping. It starts out rough and rowdy and then slows to flat water. Along the way you will see beautiful hardwood forests and farms as well as signs that this is one of the fastest-growing areas in New England. This trip should be run in spring—by the time the stream flow is below 200 cfs (check the USGS website at http://water.usgs.gov/realtime.html), it is too shallow to be runnable. No facilities are available.

The first 4.0 miles of this trip alternate between quick water, Class I rapids, and Class II rapids, with the most difficult rapids encountered during the first 1.0 mile of the trip. The section between the Blake Road bridge (0.6 mile from the put-in) and the Main Street bridge (3.6 miles) is one of the most scenic parts of the entire river. It includes some recently protected shoreline purchased by the Society for the Protection of New Hampshire Forests, where hemlocks and hardwoods such as silver maple and hophornbeam shade the riverbanks. Once you pass under NH 125 at the 4.0-mile

The wild and scenic Lamprey River.

mark, you have completed all the whitewater on the trip. The final 3.0 miles of the trip is flatwater paddling that winds past low hills on the way to the take-out at NH 87.

Directions to Put–In

From NH 27 and NH 125 in Epping, head west on NH 27. In 3.1 miles, turn right onto Folsom Mill Road into the Mary Folsom Blair Community Park. (If you cross the river, you've gone too far.) Park at the end of the road near the baseball field. The put-in is beyond the grassy area to the right of the park sign.

Directions to Take–Out

From Folsom Mill Road, turn left onto NH 27. In 3.1 miles, turn left onto NH 125. In another 1.0 mile, turn right onto Old Hedding Road. In another 1.0 mile, turn right onto NH 87. The take-out is in 0.3 mile on the left, just beyond the bridge.

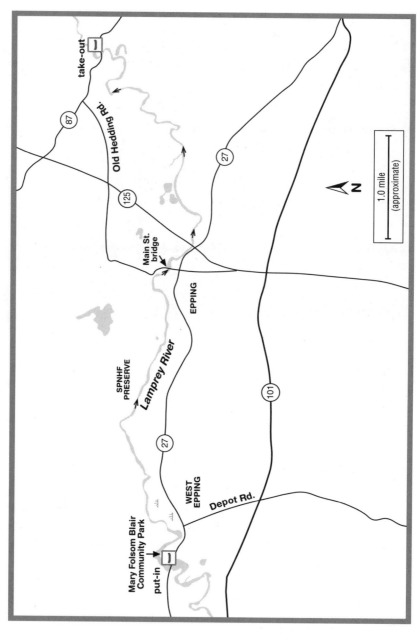

LAMPREY

take-out

Old Hedding Rd.

87

125

27

27

101

Main St.
bridge

EPPING

Lamprey River

SPNHF
PRESERVE

WEST
EPPING

Depot Rd.

Mary Folsom Blair
Community Park
put-in

N

1.0 mile
(approximate)

National Wild and Scenic Rivers System

IN 1968 THE U.S. CONGRESS passed the National Wild and Scenic Rivers Act, establishing a system for protecting free-flowing rivers with "outstandingly remarkable scenic, recreational, geologic, fish and wildlife, historic, cultural or other similar values." The first river to become part of the system was the Middle Fork of Idaho's Clearwater River. Currently more than 11,000 miles of 160 rivers are designated as part of

Packer's Falls on the Lamprey River.

the National Wild and Scenic River System. Designation does not mean a river and its shoreline become protected government property, but dam building is prohibited and certain types of streamside development can be limited and growth managed. Current levels of recreational access are also guaranteed and managed. While all designated rivers are called "Wild and Scenic," there are actually three different designations:

1. A "Wild" river has predominantly inaccessible shorelines and represents a "vestige of primitive America."

2. A "Scenic" river is primitive for the most part, but with some road access.

3. A "Recreational" river is accessible by roads and may have some streamside development.

In 1996, 11.5 miles of New Hampshire's Lamprey River were designated a recreational river under the National Wild and Scenic River System. An additional 12 miles were designated in 1999, so that now the entire river from Epping to the Piscassic River in Newmarket is considered "Wild and Scenic." As southern New Hampshire faces tremendous growth, the Lamprey's designation will help keep the river popular among boaters, anglers, and wildlife watchers. The river is also home to more than 300 species of plants and supports at least 12 plant and animal species on the state's endangered list, including spotted turtles, brook floater mussels, and ospreys.

Wildcat Brook in Jackson is New Hampshire's only other National Wild and Scenic River, although the state has designated stretches of twelve rivers as "rivers to be protected for their outstanding natural and cultural resources." Several of these are in this chapter—the Connecticut, Merrimack, Piscataquog, and Souhegan. These rivers are also potential candidates for National Wild and Scenic status if the local communities feel compelled to work toward this designation. More information about protecting rivers under the national system can be found at the American Rivers website, www.amrivers.org/default.htm, and at the National Park Service's website, www.nps.gov/rivers/. Information about the New Hampshire Rivers Management and Protection Program can be found at www.des.state.nh.us/rivers/.

Lower Winnipesaukee River

> Difficulty: **Class II**
>
> Distance: **4.5 miles**
>
> Estimated Time: **2¹/₂ hours**
>
> Maps: **USGS Northfield Quadrangle**
>
> **A flatwater lake paddle followed by some easy Class II that is runnable throughout the summer.**

THE LOWER SECTION OF THE WINNIPESAUKEE RIVER in Tilton is a relatively easy Class II paddle. While this trip starts with 2.5 miles of flatwater paddling, the final 2.0 miles are notable because they can often be run in summer when most other Class II rivers in the state are out of runnable water. A series of dams above the river keep water flowing all year long, though it can still get pretty bony in an extremely dry year. Check the USGS website (http://water.usgs.gov/realtime.html) for flow levels—a reading above 250 cfs means the river can be run, although at 250 the water is fairly slow and the rocks are numerous. Above 400 cfs, the river has some interesting features that make this an enjoyable run. No facilities are available.

From the put-in, paddle across Silver Lake, which is surprisingly clean and quiet given the number of houses on its shore. We saw tree swallows, kingbirds, great blue herons, and kingfishers on the lake, which has a sandy bottom that is home to freshwater mussels and snails. The south end of the lake is split in two by a peninsula—stay to the right to find the river. Once on the river, the houses disappear as you enter a marshy area with a number of duck-hunting blinds. In this part of the river there are more swallows and kingbirds, picking insects off the surface of the water that is full of

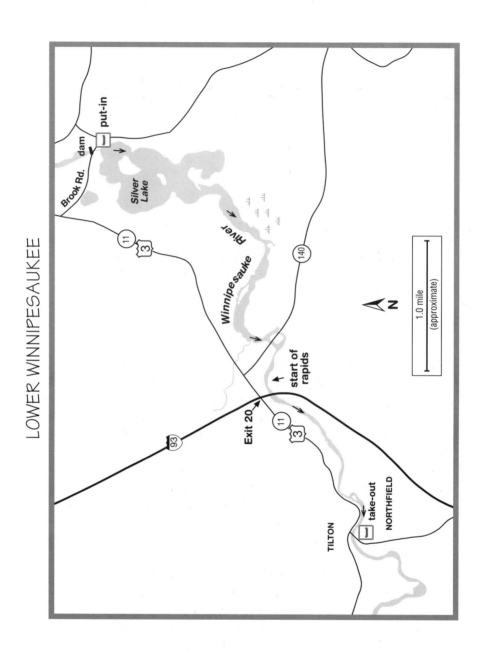

pickerelweed, water lilies, and purple loosestrife, a non-native, invasive plant that is choking out native vegetation.

After about 2.5 miles, you pass under the NH 140 bridge, where the water quickens considerably. After passing under I-93, you hit the first stretch of rapids—Class I and easy Class II. From here to the take-out, the river alternates between quick water and Class II, with the trickiest spot being a right-hand turn under a railroad trestle—aim for the middle span. The take-out will be on river left, just before the dam in Tilton.

Directions to Put-In

Take Exit 20 off I-93 and head north on US 3. In 1.8 miles, turn right onto Brook Road. The put-in is in 0.5 mile on the right in a parking area next to an electrical transformer and a dam on Silver Lake.

Directions to Take-Out

Head back to US 3 and turn left. In 3.5 miles, you reach Tilton; turn left before the statue in the center of town. After crossing the river, turn right onto Elm Street. In about 0.2 mile, turn left onto Park Street. Take the first right in about 50 yards onto an unnamed street. Cross the railroad tracks and park at the end of the street beyond some old railroad cars.

Sugar River

> **Difficulty: Class II with one Class III drop**
> **Distance: 3.3 miles**
> **Estimated Time: 2¹/₂ hours**
> **Maps: USGS Newport and Sunapee Quadrangles**
>
> **An exciting Class II run with one challenging Class III drop.**

THE SUGAR RIVER IS A POPULAR CLASS II TRIP that is often run as part of the·New Hampshire AMC's spring whitewater school. It is best run in April or early May, when the water is still high. This river is runnable when the gauge reading is between 2 and 4. The gauge is located on a rock ledge in West Claremont, but is difficult to find. Luckily, the water levels can also be found online at the USGS website, http://water.usgs.gov/realtime.html. Sweet Tooth rapid is a tough, Class III run of about 30 yards that marks the halfway point of the trip. Its combination of big rocks and turbulence can easily trip up inexperienced paddlers, but it is easily portaged. No facilities are available.

The Sugar is a great early-season run because it starts with easy Class I rapids and gradually builds in difficulty on the way to Sweet Tooth. The scenery is good, too, with high banks covered in hardwoods, white pines, and hemlocks. By the time you pass under a railroad bridge at 0.8 mile, it is a very technical Class II run, with rocks all over the river creating obstacles as well as fun river features such as eddies, waves, and small holes. At higher water levels, the river gets quite pushy and requires a fair amount of concentration. At about 1.7 miles, the river widens and makes a wide right-hand turn; there is a high bank covered in hemlocks on the left. This turn marks the beginning of Sweet Tooth rapid. The scouting/portage trail

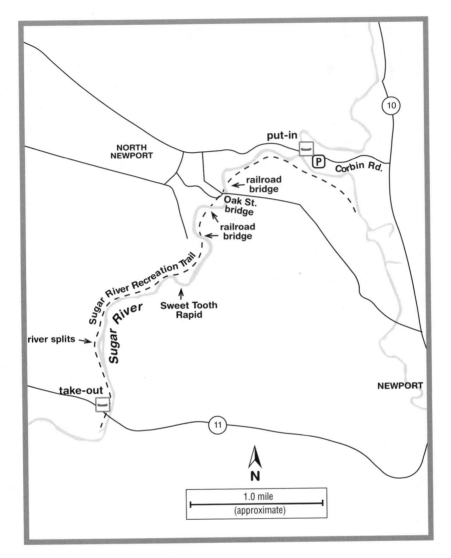

SUGAR RIVER

is on river right just before this turn—scouting is highly recommended. It is relatively easy to take the main channel past the first set of large rocks, but then a quick turn in either direction is needed to avoid turbulence associated with some additional submerged rocks.

Maneuvering through the Sugar River's Class III "Sweet Tooth" Rapid.

Beyond Sweet Tooth, the river continues its technical Class II nature. About 0.5 mile from the take-out, the river is split in the middle by a large island—either channel can be run. The take-out will be on the right, just before the NH 11 bridge in Kelleyville.

Directions to Put-In

From the intersection of NH 10 and NH 11 in Newport, head north on NH 10. In 2.1 miles, turn left onto Corbin Road. The put-in is on the left in 0.6 mile, just before the covered bridge.

Directions to Take-Out

Head back to NH 10 and turn right. In 2.1 miles, turn right onto NH 11. In 3.1 miles, cross the river and turn right onto a dirt driveway that leads down to the river.

Trip #48

Souhegan River

Difficulty: Class II

Distance: 4.5 miles

Estimated Time: 3 hours

Maps: USGS Greenville and Milford Quadrangles

One of the first Class II runs in New Hampshire to open up after winter.

THE SOUHEGAN IS OFTEN RUNNABLE when other Class II runs in the state are blocked by ice, and it has good scenery: the forest on the right bank is adjacent to the Russell-Abbott State Forest. Because the Souhegan thaws out before other rivers, it is tempting to paddle on it before it is safe—scout the river for ice shelves jutting out from the banks. Stay off the river if there is not a safe route to shore along its entire length. Ice aside, the Souhegan provides a difficult Class III run about a mile upstream from this trip, which starts below a bridge on NH 31 in Greenville. This trip is an easy Class II that is best run when the river is above the 2 mark on the gauge, located on river left on the downstream side of the bridge at the put-in. It can be run down to Min Level, but you might find it a little scratchy. No facilities are available.

The trip starts out with rocky Class II rapids on a streambed that is only about 25 feet across. The hardest rapids are found within the first 2.0 miles as the river moves swiftly through sharp turns that usually have an obstacle or two requiring quick maneuvers in pushy water. The biggest troublemaker is Bang Rock, a large rock that juts out from the right bank just as the river turns sharply left about 1.5 miles from the put-in. The Class II rapids continue as you reach an island at 2.5 miles—either side is navigable. While there are no big features on this stretch of river, wave trains and small holes (and

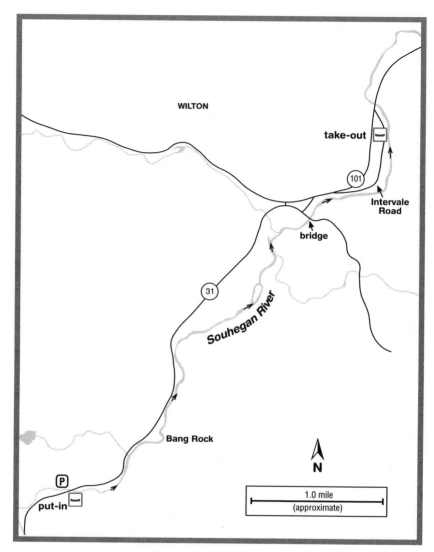

SOUHEGAN

the occasional beaver dam) make for a fun ride. The river eases up to Class I and quick water after passing under a bridge at 3.3 miles. The take-out is up a high bank on the left about 1.2 miles beyond this bridge. You can also take out at the NH 31 bridge in about another 200 yards.

Directions to Put-In

From the southernmost intersection of NH 101 and NH 31 in Wilton, head south on NH 31. Park on the shoulder just before a bridge 2.9 miles from NH 101. The put-in is on the left side of the road on river left.

Directions to Take-Out

Head back to NH 31 and NH 101 and turn right onto NH 101. In 0.6 mile, turn right onto Intervale Road. The take-out is on the right next to a 200-yard stretch of undeveloped riverfront, about 0.6 mile from NH 101.

Mink and Otter: Fish–Eating Fur Bearers

IF YOU SPEND ENOUGH TIME on and around water in New Hampshire, you are likely to encounter minks and river otters, either patrolling the shore or swimming in the water. Both feed on fish, frogs, crayfish, and shellfish, while mink will also eat ducks, mice, and other mammals as large as muskrats. They are members of the mustelid family of mammals, which also includes weasels, fishers, martens, wolverines, ferrets, skunks, and badgers; animals with long slender bodies, short legs, small rounded ears, and anal scent glands. With the exception of sea otters, minks and river otters are the only mustelids that go fishing on a regular basis. (Fishers actually stick to land-based meals such as red squirrels and berries.) Both mink and river otter are prized for their fur, and with a license it is still legal to trap both animals in New Hampshire, from late October through early April.

Minks are about 2 feet long with dark brown fur and a white patch on their chin. Males are usually a little bigger than females. They are primarily solitary and nocturnal animals, so you are most likely to see them around sunrise and sunset. Minks mate in the winter; females bear litters of one to eight baby minks in April or May, with the young staying with Mom until the following fall. Minks may not be as playful as their otter cousins, but they are still a joy to watch as they hop around the shoreline, swim across a stream, or roll around on a log marking their territory. It is hard to imagine wearing one as a coat after watching them alertly cruising a riverbank in search of a morning meal.

River otters are easy to distinguish from minks, as they are much larger—up to 4 feet in length—and while they have dark brown fur on their backs, they have an obvious silvery sheen underneath. You are also more likely to see an otter in the water than on land, often telescoping its head up above the water like a periscope. Otters breed in early spring, with

A mink scouts its surroundings.

one to five pups being born ten to twelve months later. The
female usually chases the male away soon after birth, but he
often returns at a later date to help care for the young. They
tend to live in pairs and family groups, and they regularly
seem to be playing—sliding down riverbanks, burrowing
through snow, and chasing each other. Their playful actions
and round faces with big eyes, long whiskers, and small round
ears make them a favorite of wildlife watchers.

Minks and river otters are both doing relatively well in
New Hampshire at present. The fur market affects their populations less now than in the past, and the waterways in the
state are much cleaner. Both are still at risk from pollution,
however—especially mercury, which is present in all New
Hampshire fresh water due to airborne pollutants discharged
from power plants and incinerators to the west. Habitat loss
is also a major concern, because shorelines are regularly
developed for homes and vacation cottages.

Suncook River

Difficulty: **Class II**

Distance: **5.5 miles**

Estimated Time: **3 hours**

Maps: **USGS Pittsfield Quadrangle**

5.5 miles of playful water and great scenery.

THE SUNCOOK RIVER DRAINS the group of lakes just south of the Belknap Range and flows about 30 miles to the Merrimack between Concord and Manchester. It is a relatively small river, but during spring runoff it provides a great Class II run from Pittsfield to Chichester. There is no gauge for this river, but you can get an idea of how it is running at the put-in and by taking a look at the rapids below the Websters Mill bridge. In very high water, the rapids in the 0.25 mile before this bridge are difficult Class II, with one very large wave that can swamp open boats. Scout these rapids ahead of time and do not attempt to run them if water levels are high unless you have experience in Class III water. The road to the bridge heads east from NH 28, about 1.0 mile south of Pittsfield. No facilities are available.

From the put-in below the Pittsfield dam, the river begins as easy Class II and passes some houses before taking on a wilder feel. It meanders past very high banks with hemlocks and pines. Depending on the water level, the river will either be very rocky or very wavy as it alternates between quick water, Class I, and Class II. Mergansers are common, and the occasional beaver lodge juts out from shore. After about 2.5 miles, the river makes a ninety-degree left turn; the bank on the right is about 150 feet high. After this left turn you soon hit the rapids before the Websters Mill bridge, starting with a pushy, tight S-turn that is followed by a ledge extending across the

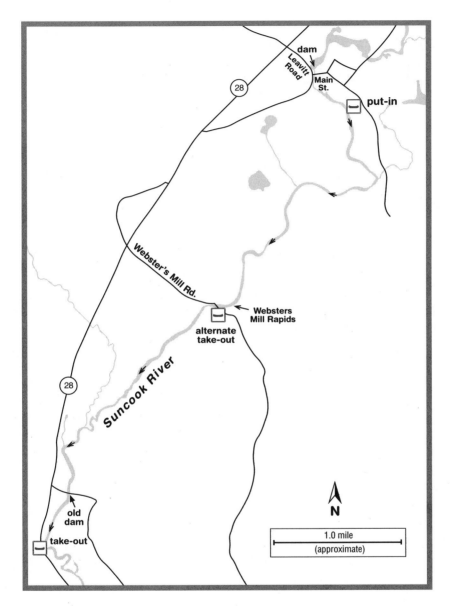

SUNCOOK RIVER

entire river. This is the ledge that creates the big wave in high water. After this ledge, there are a few big rocks to dodge before you pass under the bridge.

Now a few Class II wave trains offer some decent play spots, depending on the water level. After these wave trains, the rapids end and you can enjoy a lazy quickwater pace for the rest of the paddle as you pass through pastoral southern New Hampshire scenery. About 0.5 mile before the take-out, you will pass under a pair of bridges at Gosboro Road and then over an old dam. In high water, you will barely notice the ripple as you pass over the dam, but in lower water, you may need to scout this feature before running it. The take-out will be on your right as you approach the Lazy River campground.

Directions to Put–In

From NH 28 in Pittsfield, head east on Leavitt Road toward downtown. In 0.3 mile, turn left onto Main Street. Cross the dam on Main Street and then take the first right. Park next to the large propane tank on the right in about 0.3 mile.

Directions to Take–Out

Head back to NH 28 (Suncook Valley Road) and turn left, heading south. Park on the left shoulder across the river from the Lazy River Campground, 3.6 miles south of Leavitt Road.

Directions to Alternate Take–Out

From Pittsfield, drive south on NH 28. About 1.0 mile south of Leavitt Road, turn left on Webster Mill Road. Cross the river in another 0.5 mile, where the take-out is on the left.

South Branch of the Piscataquog River

> Difficulty: **Class II**
> Distance: **6.5 miles**
> Estimated Time: **3¹/₂ hours**
> Maps: **USGS New Boston and Weare Quadrangles**
>
> **A technical Class II paddle through forests and historic New Boston.**

A REGULAR ON THE NEW HAMPSHIRE AMC'S early-spring trip list, the South Branch of the Piscataquog River is a fun paddle with plenty of rocks to dodge on its way to a wavy twist through the center of New Boston. It is a small river that must be run in March or early April when the water is high enough to float a kayak or canoe. There is one small dam that requires a short portage about a third of the way through the trip, but the dam in the center of New Boston has been breached and is easily runnable in high water. There is no gauge for this river. No facilities are available.

From the put-in, there are about 1.5 miles of Class I rapids before you pass under Lyndenboro Road and begin a stretch of Class II rapids that lasts until just before the dam at 2.5 miles. The short portage trail is on river right. The portage will give you a chance to admire the stonework of the dam as well as the maples, hemlocks, and mountain laurel on the banks. There are a few hundred yards of Class II below the dam before the whitewater eases up a bit as the river snakes its way through the forest and then passes under the first of two NH 13 bridges at 3.0 miles. The river's pace soon quickens after this bridge: there is another set of Class II rapids as you pass through the center of New Boston and under NH 13 once again.

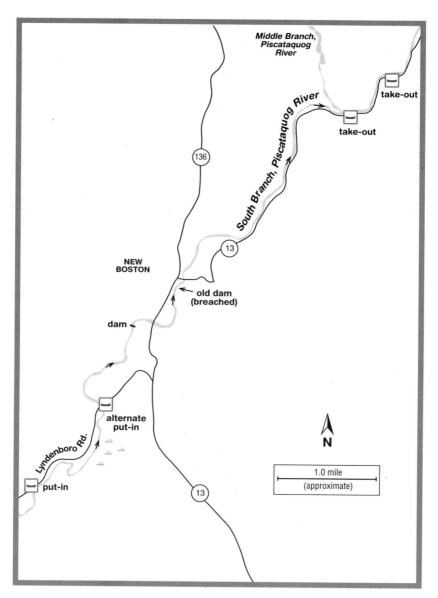

SOUTH BRANCH OF THE PISCATAQUOG

There can be some big waves in high water as you pass over the old dam and under NH 13 at 3.5 miles on what is probably the most exciting section of the river.

After passing through New Boston, the river alternates between Class I rapids and quick water as it winds its way through forests and past houses. Rocks provide an occasional obstacle, but the only real risk on this section is strainers. It would make sense to scout this area ahead of time from NH 13. While NH 13 is close by, it seldom intrudes on the experience of paddling through the hardwood forest as you wind down from the adventures of paddling the whitewater earlier in the trip.

Directions to Put-In

From the intersection of NH 136 and NH 13 in New Boston, head south on NH 13. In 1.1 miles, turn right onto Lyndeboro Road. You cross a bridge (and the alternate put-in) in another 0.6 mile. The put-in is 1.6 miles from this bridge on the left—walk about 20 yards on the well-trodden path through the pines.

Directions to Take-Out

Head back to the intersection of NH 136 and NH 13. Turn right to stay on NH 13, which then crosses the river in the center of New Boston and turns left. There are numerous pullouts on the left side of NH 13 that can be used as take-outs. Two of the best spots are about 3 miles and 3.5 miles north of New Boston.

9
other activities

I N CASE YOU DON'T FEEL LIKE HIKING, biking, or paddling the whole time you are visiting southern New Hampshire, there is plenty more for you to do.

Amusement Parks

- *Fun Spot*—Weirs Beach; 603-366-4377; www.funspotnh.com. Fun Spot offers new and classic video games, a twenty-lane ten-pin and candlepin bowling center, cash bingo, mini-golf, a driving range, a new indoor golf center, and more.

- *Surfcoaster USA*—Weirs Beach; 603-366-5600; www.surfcoasterusa.com. Surfcoaster USA occupies more than eleven acres of land and contains nine different attractions: six water slides, a 700-foot winding tube ride, a 500,000-gallon wave pool, and a large separate area for children.

- *Water Country*—Portsmouth; 603-427-1111; www.watercountry.com. New England's largest water park. Many thrill-seeker rides, but also relaxing rides such as

Adventure River and the Whirlpool. There is a huge wave pool and many rides designed just for kids.

Boat Cruises

Seacoast Region

- *Isles of Shoals Steamship Co.*—Portsmouth; 603-431-5500; www.islesofshoals.com. Cruises all around the seacoast, including island and harbor tours, whale watching, evening cruises, fall foliage specials, and lighthouse cruises.

- *Buccaneer Charters*—Portsmouth; 603-431-6999; www.buccaneercharters.com. Dive charters, evening cruises, trips to Isles of Shoals, kayak transport, and Down East–style clambakes.

- *Portsmouth Harbor Cruises*—Portsmouth; 603-436-8084; www.portsmouthharbor.com. Harbor tours, Isles of Shoals cruises, inland river and fall foliage tours.

Lakes Region

- *Golden Pond Tours*—Holderness; 603-968-7194; www.nhnature.org. Beautiful cruise on Squam Lake.

- *M/S Mount Washington*—Weirs Beach; 888-THE-MOUNT; www.cruisenh.com. Scenic cruise on Lake Winnipesaukee, New Hampshire's largest lake.

Museums and Historic Sites

Seacoast Region

- *Children's Museum of Portsmouth*—603-436-3853; www.childrens-museum.org. Hand-on exhibits designed for learning and fun include computers, dinosaurs, literature, music, and world cultures.

- *Strawbery Banke Museum*—Portsmouth; 603-433-1100; www.strawberybanke.org. Explore the Portsmouth neighborhood known for 400 years as Puddle Dock. Visit historic houses all set in different times from the 1600s to the 1950s.

Dartmouth–Sunapee Region

- *Mount Kearsarge Indian Museum*—Warner; 603-456-2600; www.indianmuseum.org. New Hampshire's only museum devoted exclusively to Native American culture.

Merrimack Valley Region

- *The Currier Gallery of Art*—Manchester; 603-669-6144; www.currier.org. An internationally renowned art museum featuring European and American paintings, decorative arts, and sculptures.

- *Christa McAuliffe Planetarium*—Concord; 603-271-7831; www.starhop.com. Explore astronomy and space science in this planetarium erected in memory of Christa McAuliffe. Spectacular multimedia shows.

- *Museum of New Hampshire History*—Concord; 603-226-3189; www.NHHistory.org. Hands-on exhibits tell New Hampshire's story from Native American times to today.

Science and Nature Centers

- *Loon Center*—Moultonboro; 603-476-5666; www.loon.org. Open six days a week year-round and seven days a week from July 1 to Columbus Day. Displays, exhibits, award-winning videos, and interpretive talks introduce visitors to the wonders of New Hampshire's environment and wildlife.

- *Newfound Audubon Center*—Hebron; 603-744-3516. This Audubon Center has fantastic programs and exhibits and lovely nature trails to go exploring.

- *Science Center of New Hampshire*—Holderness; 603-968-7194. A 200-acre facility offering an exhibit of live animals, interactive bird exhibit, children's center, and nature cruises on Squam Lake. Open May through November.

- *Seacoast Science Center*—Rye; 603-436-8043; www.seacentr.org. The center offers year-round programs, including naturalist-guided or unguided explorer programs for schools, visitor programs on the natural and social history of Odiorne Point and the Gulf of Maine, and a variety of indoor exhibits highlighting some of the fascinating features of coastal New Hampshire. Lovely trails lead through the woods and along the ocean.

- *Stonedam Island Natural Area*—across from Weirs, Meredith; 603-279-7278. Self-guided nature trails are the centerpiece of this nature center, which focuses on conservation programs. Educational events are scheduled at the site throughout the season. Open July through Labor Day.

Scuba Diving

- *Portsmouth Scuba*—Portsmouth; 603-436-4887; www.portsmouthscuba.com. Take a class or have them charter you out to the Isles of Shoals.

Train Ride

- *Winnipesaukee Scenic Railroad*—Meredith; 603-279-5253; www.hoborr.com. Enjoy a scenic ride along Lake Winnipesaukee.

Tourist Attractions

- *America's Stonehenge*—Salem; 603-893-8300; www.stonehengeusa.com. A maze of artificially constructed chambers, walls, and ceremonial meeting places, America's Stonehenge is one of the oldest constructions in the United States. Built by a Native American culture or a migrant European population? No one knows for sure.

- *Canterbury Shaker Village*—Canterbury; 603-783-9511; www.shakers.org. Take a step back in time and experience 200 years of the Shaker way of life. Visit this National Historic Landmark with twenty-five original buildings situated on a rolling hilltop surrounded by open fields, woodlots, and ponds. A guided tour will introduce the customs, inventions, furniture, architecture, and values of this utopian society. Watch crafts being made in the Shaker tradition. Explore the Physician's Botanical Garden and three easily accessible nature trails to millponds, archaeological remains of old mills, and dam sites—694 acres in all.

- *Ruggles Mine*—Grafton; 603-523-4275; www.rugglesmine.com. The oldest, most spectacular mica, feldspar, and beryl mine in the nation. More than 150 minerals are found, and collecting is permitted.

- *Enfield Shaker Museum*—*Enfield*; 603-632-7810; www.shakermuseum.org. thirteen shaker buildings on over 1,100 acres of Shaker fields, pastures, and forests. The museum includes exhibition galleries, photographic exhibits, crafts demonstrations, children's activities, and a self-guided walking tour.

Whale Watching

- **Al Gauron Deep Sea Fishing & Whale Watching:** State Pier, Hampton Beach; 800-905-7820; www.whalewatching-nh.com.

- **Atlantic Queen II:** Rye; 1-800-WHALE-NH; www.atlanticwhalewatch.com.

- **Eastman's Fishing Fleet, Inc.:** Seabrook; 603-474-3461; www.eastmansdocks.com.

- **Granite State Whale Watch:** Rye; 800-964-5545; www.whale-rye.com.

- **Smith & Gilmore:** Ocean Boulevard, Hampton Beach; 877-272-4005; www.smithandgilmore.com.

recommended reading

Guidebooks

Burroughs, Jon, and Gene Daniell. *Southern New Hampshire Trail Guide*. Appalachian Mountain Club, 1999.

Demrow, Carl, and David Salisbury. *The Complete Guide to Trail Building and Maintenance*. Appalachian Mountain Club, 1998.

Jas, Victoria. *Appalachian Mountain Club River Guide—New Hampshire/Vermont, 3rd ed.*. Appalachian Mountain Club, 2002.

Lessels, Bruce. *Classic Northeastern Whitewater Guide: The Best Whitewater Runs in New England and New York—Novice to Expert*. Appalachian Mountain Club, 1998.

Lessels, Bruce and Karen. *Paddling with Kids*. Appalachian Mountain Club, 2002.

U'ren, Stephen B. *Performance Kayaking*. Stackpole Books, 1990.

Wilson, Alex. *Appalachian Mountain Club Quiet Water Canoe & Kayak Guide—New Hampshire/Vermont, 2nd ed.*: Appalachian Mountain Club, 2001.

History/Stories

Brown, Dona. *A Tourist's New England: Travel Fiction 1820–1920*. University Press of New England, 1999.

Cronon, William. *Changes in the Land: Indians, Colonists, and the Ecology of New England*. Hill and Wang, 1983.

Ober, Richard. *At What Cost? Shaping the Land We Call New Hampshire. A Land Use History*. The New Hampshire Historical Society and the Society for the Protection of New Hampshire Forests, 1992.

Stier, Maggie, and Ron McAdow. *Into the Mountains: Stories of New England's Most Celebrated Peaks*. Appalachian Mountain Club, 1995.

Tougias, Michael. *River Days: Exploring the Connecticut River from Source to Sea*. Appalachian Mountain Club, 2001.

Waterman, Laura, and Guy Waterman. *Forest and Crag: A History of Hiking, Trail Blazing, and Adventure in the Northeast Mountains*. Appalachian Mountain Club, 1989.

Wilson, James. *The Earth Shall Weep: A History of Native America*. Grove Press, 1998.

Nature

Taylor, James, Thomas D. Lee, and Laura Falk McCarthy. *New Hampshire's Living Legacy: The Biodiversity of the Granite State*. New Hampshire Fish and Game Department Nongame and Endangered Wildlife Program, 1996.

VanDiver, Bradford. *Roadside Geology of Vermont and New Hampshire*. Mountain Press, 1987.

Waterman, Laura, and Guy Waterman. *Backwoods Ethics: Environmental Issues for Hikers and Campers*. Countryman Press, 1993.

Wessels, Tom. *Reading the Forested Landscape: A Natural History of New England*. Countryman Press, 1997.

nonprofit conservation organizations

Appalachian Mountain Club: 617-523-0655, www.outdoors.org

Audubon Society of New Hampshire: 603-224-9909, www.nhaudubon.org

Beaver Brook Association: 603-465-7787, www.beaverbrook.org

The Harris Center for Conservation Education: 603-525-3394

Leave No Trace: 303-442-8222, www.lnt.org

Merrimack Watershed Council: 978-681-5777, www.merrimack.org

The Nature Conservancy (NH): 603-224-5853, www.tnc.org

Rails-to-Trails Conservancy, New England: 508-755-3300, www.railtrails.org/NewEngland/

Society for the Protection of New Hampshire Forests (SPNHF): 603-224-9945, www.spnhf.org

Upper Valley Land Trust: 603-643-6626, http://www.uvlt.org

The Wilderness Society: 617-350-8866, www.wilderness.org/ccc/northeast

New England Mountain Biking Association: 800-576-3622, www.nemba.org

Trailwrights: P.O. Box 1945, Hillsboro, NH 03244, www.mv.com/ipusers/blanchette/trailwrights

Sunapee-Rugged-Kearsarge Greenway Coalition: www.nlrec.com/orgs/srkgc.htm

Monadnock-Sunapee Greenway Trail club, P.O. Box 164, Marlow, NH 03456, www.msgtc.org

American Whitewater Affiliation: 866-262-8429; www.americanwhitewater.org

The Trust for Public Lands, New England Region: 617-367-6200; www.tpl.org.

appendix c
lodging

LITERALLY HUNDREDS OF CHOICES for lodging exist in southern New Hampshire. They range from basic camprgrounds to very nice hotels and inns. Here are some resources to help you find the place that's right for your needs.

State of New Hampshire Division of tourism: 800-FUN-IN-NH, www.visitnh.gov

Seacoast Region

Information and Welcome Center: 603-474-5211

Hampton Beach Chamber of Commerce: 603-926-8718; www.hamptonbeach.org

Portsmouth Chamber of Commerce: 603-436-1118; www.portcity.org

Merrimack Valley Region

Concord Area Chamber of Commerce: 603-224-2508; www.concordnhchamber.com

Manchester Chamber of Commerce: 603-666-6600; www.manchester-chamber.org

Merrimack Chamber of Commerce: 603-424-3669; www.merrimackchamber.org

Monadnock Region

Keene Chamber of Commerce: 603-352-1303; www.keenechamber.com

Monadnock Lodging Association: www.nhlodging.org

Monadnock Travel Council: 603-355-8155; www.monadnocktravel.com

Souhegan Valley Chamber of Commerce: 603-673-4360; www.souhegan.net

Peterborough Chamber of Commerce: 603-924-7324; www.peterboroughchamber.com

Dartmouth–Sunapee Region

Hanover Chamber of Commerce: 603-643-3115; www.hanoverchamber.org

Lebanon Chamber of Commerce: 603-448-1203; www.lebanonchamber.com

New London Chamber of Commerce 603-526-6575; www.newlondonareanh.com

Sunapee Business Association: 800-258-3530; www.sunapeevacations.com

Lakes Region

Alton Bay Chamber of Commerce: 603-875-5777

Appalachian Mountain Club, Three-Mile Island, Lake Winnipesaukee: 800-262-4455, www.outdoors.org/lodging/camps/camps-threemile.shtml

Newfound Region Chamber of Commerce: 603-744-2150; www.newfoundchamber.com

Center Harbor/Moultonboro Chamber of Commerce: 603-253-5482

Squam Lake Chamber of Commerce: 603-968-4494; www.squamlakeschamber.com

Greater Laconia/Weirs Beach Chamber of Commerce: 603-524-5531; www.laconia-weirs.org

Plymouth Chamber of Commerce: 800-386-3678; www.plymouthnh.org.

Wolfeboro Chamber of Commerce: 603-569-2200; www.wolfeborochamber.com

Camping

For campground information, try these resources:

New Hampshire State Parks (also see the appendix D: 603-271-3556; www.nhparks.nh.us.com

New Hampshire Campground Owners Associations: 800-222-7444; www.koakampgrounds.com

New Hampshire Division of Tourism: 800-FUN-IN-NH; www.visitnh.gov

state parks

Name	Location	Open Season
Hampton Beach State Park	Seacoast: Route 1A, Hampton, 603-926-3784	Early May–Mid-October
Odiorne State Park	Seacoast: Route 1A, Rye, 603-436-7406	Year-round
Bear Brook State Park	Merrimack Valley: off Route 28, Allenstown, 603-485-9874	Early May–Mid-October
Northwood Meadows State Park	Merrimack Valley: off Route 4, Northwood, 603-436-1552	Year-round
Pawtuckaway State Park	Merrimack Valley: Nottingham, 603-895-3031	Early May–Mid-October
Greenfield State Park	Monadnock Region: Route 136, Greenfield, 603-547-3497	Early May–Columbus Day
Miller State Park	Monadnock Region: off Route 101, Peterborough, 603-924-3672	April–October
Monadnock State Park	Monadnock Region: off Route 124 Jaffrey, 603-532-8862	Year–round (limited winter services)
Pisgah State Park	Monadnock Region: Chesterfield, 603-239-8153	Year-round
Rhododendron State Park	Monadnock Region: Route 119W Fitzwilliam, 603-239-8153	May–Labor Day
Cardigan State Park	Dartmouth-Sunapee Region: off Route 118, Orange 603-547-3373	Year-round
Pillsbury State Park	Dartmouth-Sunapee Region: Route 31, Washington, 603-863-2860	Early May–Columbus Day
Rollins State Park	Dartmouth-Sunapee Region: off Route 103, Warner, 603-456-3808	June–October
Sunapee State Park/Beach	Dartmouth-Sunapee Region: Route 103, Newbury, 603-763-5561	June–Columbus Day
Winslow State Park	Dartmouth-Sunapee Region: off Route 11, Wilmot, 603-526-6168	Mid-May–November
Ellacoya State Park	Lakes Region: Route 11, Gilford, 603-293-7821	Early May–Mid-October
White Lake State Park	Lakes Region: Route 16, Tamworth, 603-323-7350	Mid-May–Mid-October

* Universal Accessibility:
1. Accessible with much assistance 2. Accessible with some assistan

Camping Sites	Hiking	Biking	Swimming	Boating	Fishing	Bathhouse	Universal Access*	Pets Permitted	Other
28 RV only		•		•	•		2		Store, oceanfront
0	•	•		•	•	•	3		Oceanfront, Seacoast Science Center, education programs
96	•		•		•	•	2	In the campground only	Canoe and rowboat rentals, showers, camp store, museums, campground programs
0	•	•			•		3		
193	•	•	•	•	•	•	3		Showers, store, fire tower
252			•	•	•	•	3	In the campground only	Showers, canoe rentals, store
0	•						2	•	Auto road to summit of Pack Monadnock
21	•					•	3		Store
0	•	•			•		1	•	
0	•						3		16 acres of rhododendron (bloom in mid-July)
0	•							•	
40	•	•	re-stricted	•			1	•	Canoe rentals, canoe-in campsites
0	•						2	•	
0	•	•	re-stricted	•	•		2	•	
0	•						2	•	
38 RV only			•	re-stricted	•	•	3		Sandy beach
200			•	re-stricted	•	•	3		Store, canoe rentals, showers

3. Fully accessible

kayak outfitters

Portsmouth Rent & Ride: Portsmouth, 603-433-6777,
www.portsmouthrentandride.com

Portsmouth Kayak Adventures: Portsmouth, 603-559-1000,
www.portsmouthkayak.com

Pemi-Baker River Adventures: Plymouth, 877-786-5692,
www.pbriveradventures.com

Winnipesaukee Kayak Co., Inc.: Wolfeboro, 603-569-9926,
www.winnikayak.com

index

about the authors

JERRY AND MARCY MONKMAN specialize in eco-photography, creating images that depict nature and man's interaction with nature. From their home base in Portsmouth, New Hampshire, they spend as much time as possible hiking, biking, and paddling around New England with their daughter, Acadia, capturing it all on film. Their photos of the Northeast are published regularly by the Appalachian Mountain Club, the Northern Forest Alliance, and the Trust for Public Land. Their work has also appeared in *National Geographic Adventure, Backpacker, Outdoor Photographer, Outdoor Explorer, Canoe and Kayak, Conservation Sciences, Yankee Magazine, Men's Journal,* and *Natural History*, as well as in National Audubon Society and National Geographic field guides. They maintain a website full of pictures and travel essays at www.ecophotography.com. *Discover Southern New Hampshire* is the third in their "Discover" series, following books on Acadia National Park and New Hampshire's White Mountains.

about the amc

SINCE 1876, the Appalachian Mountain Club has helped people experience the majesty and solitude of the Northeast outdoors. We offer outdoor skills workshops, guided trips, and lodging options for all levels of outdoor adventuring. Our programs include trail maintenance, air and water quality research, and conservation advocacy work to preserve the special outdoor places we love and enjoy for future generations.

Join the Club!

Take a hike, ride a bike, paddle a canoe. We believe that people who enjoy climbing mountains, splashing in streams, and walking on trails have more fun and take better care of the outdoors. Join the fun today. Call 617-523-0636 or visit www.outdoors.org for membership information. AMC members receive discounts on workshops, lodging, and books.

Outdoor Adventures

From beginner backpacking to advanced backcountry skiing to guided hiking and paddling trips, we teach outdoor skills workshops to suit your interest and experience. Our outdoor education centers guarantee year-round adventures. View our entire listing of workshops online at www.outdoors.org.

Huts, Lodges, and Visitor Centers

The Appalachian Mountain Club provides accommodations throughout the Northeast so you don't have to travel to the ends of the earth to experience unique wilderness lodging. Accessible by car or onfoot, our lodges and huts are perfect for families, couples, groups, and individuals. For reservations call 800-262-4455.

Books and Maps

We can lead you to the best hiking, biking, skiing, and paddling destinations from Maine to North Carolina. With more than fifty books and maps published, we're your definitive resource for discovering wonderful outdoor places. To receive a free catalog call 800-262-4455 or visit our online store at www.outdoors.org.

Contact Us

Appalachian Mountain Club
5 Joy Street
Boston, MA 02108-1490
617-523-0636
www.outdoors.org

leave no trace

THE APPALACHIAN MOUNTAIN CLUB is a national educational partner of Leave No Trace, a nonprofit organization dedicated to promoting and inspiring responsible outdoor recreation through education, research, and partnerships. The Leave No Trace Program seeks to develop wildland ethics— ways in which people think and act in the outdoors to minimize their impacts on the areas they visit and to protect our natural resources for future enjoyment. Leave No Trace unites four federal land management agencies—the U.S. Forest Service, National Park Service, Bureau of Land Management, and U.S. Fish and Wildlife Service— with manufacturers, outdoor retailers, user groups, educators, organizations such as the AMC and the National Outdoor Leadership School (NOLS), and individuals.

The Leave No Trace ethic is guided by these seven principles:

- Plan ahead and prepare
- Travel and camp on durable surfaces
- Dispose of waste properly
- Leave what you find
- Minimize campfire impacts
- Respect wildlife
- Be considerate of other visitors

The AMC has joined NOLS—a recognized leader in wilderness education and a founding partner of Leave No Trace—as the only sole national providers of the Leave No Trace Master Educator course through 2004. The AMC offers this five-day course, designed especially for outdoor professionals and land managers, as well as the shorter two-day Leave No Trace Trainer course, at locations throughout the Northeast.

For Leave No Trace information and materials contact:

Leave No Trace, P.O. Box 997, Boulder, CO 80306; 800-332-4100; www.LNT.org